The
Failed
Experiment

Andrew Fisher

First published in Great Britain in 2014
By Comerford and Miller
Under their A Radical Read Imprint
36 Grosvenor Road,
West Wickham,
BR4 9PY

http://www.radicalread.co.uk

info@radicalread.co.uk

ISBN 978-1-871204-28-5

British Library Cataloguing in Publication Data is available
from the British Library

Printed in the UK by Tyson Media Herons Way Chester CH4 9QR

Cover design Swatt-design Eastleigh, Hampshire
Typeset Robbie Griffiths

The graph on the cover is not plotted against any known data;
it is purely symbolic to demonstrate the 2008 financial crash
and the uncertainty that has followed it.

Contents

To my son Micah, and all who deserve a better world.

Acknowledgements

This book has taken longer to write than I had expected. Much of that delay was caused by the birth of my first child, Micah John Fisher, born in March 2013. This book is dedicated to him and his wonderful mum Lucy, who I have no doubt neglected at times to get this book completed.

I must also thank my publisher Comerford & Miller, especially Russell Miller and Ted Knight, for their immense patience and continued faith in me despite the delays. I hope this book justifies their faith.

The idea for this book was developed from a lecture I was invited to give at a Labour History conference in October 2012, so thanks must also go to Stan Newens and John Kotz for inviting me to address that meeting – and to all those who attended and joined the debate afterwards.

Just as the concept for a book is a team effort, even more so is the writing. I am grateful to friends, family and colleagues for their comments, criticisms and assistance in reading early drafts and greatly improving the final text that you are now reading. Thank you Amanda Fisher, John Fisher, John McDonnell, Enrico Tortolano, and Dave Watson.

Thanks must also go to those people willing to be interviewed for the book, and who answered questions and gave insights about some of the more complex issues raised in it: Bryn Davies, John McDonnell MP, and Professor Prem Sikka – as well as the countless people whose innovative ideas, campaigning zeal, and great writing have inspired me over several years of political and economic thinking.

Introduction

In my lifetime an economic consensus emerged that I call the 'great experiment'. It began roughly with the election of the Thatcher government just seven months before I was born. The 'great experiment' had failed spectacularly by 2008.

In the years since 'the credit crunch' we have witnessed a scene that would have graced Monty Python. In a manner reminiscent of the 'Dead Parrot' sketch politicians have told us that the economy created in the 'great experiment' has not failed, and they will revive it.

The financial crash of 2008 was not caused by Gordon Brown employing too many nurses, by civil service pensions being too large or by unemployment benefit being too generous. Like successive governments for the last three decades the last Labour government cannot escape its responsibility for perpetuating an unsound political doctrine; a folly that has had disastrous consequences.

Since the crash, there has been a sterile consensus that we had no alternative to bailing out the banks in 2008, starting quantitative easing in 2009 and austerity since 2010. This book identifies the political causes of the economic crisis over a generation and ends by offering solutions – to build an economy in our interests, as if people mattered.

The more we understand how our economy works, the better we can argue for and build a better one.

The economy is not a force of nature. It is shaped by all of us and is framed by the political choices of governments. With different political decisions the economic crisis could have been prevented. With different political choices now the crisis can be resolved, and a better society created.

1

The financial crash – what happened?

Northern Rock

On Friday 14 September 2007, people awoke to news coverage of the strange sight of long queues forming outside of Northern Rock branches across the UK. Its customers had heard the bank required emergency funding, and feared it was on the brink of collapse. They wanted to get their money out.

This was the first run on a bank since the nineteenth century. A bank run is caused by large numbers of customers withdrawing their deposits leaving the bank without sufficient liquidity. Think of liquidity as the money you get from the cash point for your day-to-day purchases. If you no longer have access to cash, you are without liquidity. If you hold assets like a house or a car, these enable you to get a loan – to borrow against your assets (known as collateral when used to secure a loan) and gain liquidity that way. No one would lend Northern Rock money anymore. Other banks did not believe the Rock had reliable assets, hence why its only option was to go to the lender of last resort, the Bank of England.

News that Northern Rock had gone to the Bank of England spooked not only Northern Rock's customers, but also its shareholders and potential investors. It was a clear admission that the bank was in trouble. It was therefore unsurprising that Northern Rock's share price plummeted that day – losing a third of its value after it begged the Bank of England for emergency funding. It was almost immediately clear that something had gone very wrong at Northern Rock. What was surprising was the knock-on effect. Shares in nearly every other UK bank started falling too. This in itself deserves some consideration. If a rival company goes bust that is generally good news for its competitors – they increase their market share, and can expect an upturn. When rival companies' shares start falling as well, it is an indication that the problem is systemic, rather than the failing of a few individual companies.

Before we look at the systemic failings of the banking sector, it's important to understand what caused the failure of Northern Rock. It wasn't that its customers withdrew their deposits – even though they withdrew an estimated £1 billion in a single day. They did that because they learned that earlier in the week the bank had gone cap in hand to the Bank of England for emergency funding. People are understandably concerned when banks – which might hold every penny they own – need emergency funding. Northern Rock account holders' fears proved to be well-founded when the bank finally did collapse, although most people's modest deposits would have been protected anyway through the financial services compensation scheme (FSCS) established in 2001, which would have protected up to £35,000 in their accounts.[1]

Northern Rock was the UK's first and most visually spectacular banking collapse of the global financial crash. Until 1997, it had been a building society. Building societies had emerged in England in the late eighteenth century, as a means of pooling funds to finance house building for the members of the building society. As we will see, Northern Rock had moved a long way from such modest beginnings.

When it became a bank, Northern Rock aggressively grew its mortgage lending activity to become one of the five biggest mortgage lenders shortly before its collapse. It offered 125%

mortgages to borrowers, something few other banks did, and it did so on a scale like no other. By the time of its collapse Northern Rock was responsible for just under one-fifth of UK lending. Within six months of the Rock's collapse, the few other lenders that had offered 125% mortgages had withdrawn them.

When it crashed, and required a public bailout, the complexity of Northern Rock was laid bare – but it was by no means clear for all to see. The bank had established a group of structured investment vehicles (SIVs) called Granite (a witty play on words) which were based in Jersey, a tax haven or secrecy jurisdiction. Granite was ultimately owned by a charitable trust, for the benefit of disabled children in the north east of England, and this trust held Northern Rock's mortgages. There is no evidence that even one penny ever went to benefit any disabled children in the north east (or anywhere else).

Granite securitised Northern Rock's assets (its customers' mortgage debts). Securitisation is the process of selling mortgages in the financial markets to raise money. The purchaser lends money to the seller (Granite) and is then repaid by the debtor (the mortgage holder). Northern Rock was therefore exchanging assets (mortgage accounts) for cash (loans). When the credit crunch hit, and banks were more suspicious of the real value of each other's assets, the model failed as Northern Rock could not raise sufficient liquidity (cash) to continue lending and make good on its repayment promises.

Northern Rock did not sell the mortgages to Granite, but just 'assigned' them. Mortgage holders knew nothing of the arrangement. They made their mortgage payments to Northern Rock – and Northern Rock paid all but a small handling fee over to Granite, which held and then sold the mortgages. Granite securitised mortgages to raise capital (i.e. get loans) to lend to Northern Rock. Northern Rock used this money to offer more mortgages, and so the cycle continued.

Problems arose when, following the subprime crisis in the US in 2006/07, investors became wary of the real value of Northern Rock's and other banks' assets. Without the ability of Granite to feed money through to Northern Rock, the bank could not offer more mortgages. Without the ready cash Northern Rock could not pay its loans or meet its other obligations.

Granite existed in the legal netherworld of Jersey's secretive and the UK's lightly regulated financial systems. Granite (and the assets it held) was listed in Northern Rock's accounts, but when the bank was nationalised (bailed-out with public money) Granite was considered legally separate. As the chartered accountant and tax justice campaigner Richard Murphy explained:

> "[Granite]'s officially 'on' its balance sheet in its accounts. But it is legally 'off' its balance sheet when it comes to getting hold of its assets as the basis for the security of the sums owed the Treasury: these assets are instead already beholden to others."[2]

Northern Rock could not have operated without Granite, which was an integral part of its business operation. Granite – based in Jersey – had no employees and no offices. Its existence as an independent entity was a charade. In truth it was wholly administered by Northern Rock.

Company accounts have to be independently audited each year and, at the end of February 2007, Northern Rock's annual accounts had been signed off unqualified (meaning without reservation) by their auditors PricewaterhouseCoopers. In July, just six weeks before the bank run, the auditors also signed off the bank's interim accounts for the six months until 30 June 2007.[3]

Companies appoint their own auditors, which are themselves other private companies. Northern Rock's auditors were also acting as consultants to Northern Rock management. This is the reality of the current arrangement – auditors are paid by the banks and depend upon their satisfaction for continued work. They are independent in the sense that they are a legally independent business, but are utterly dependent on the goodwill of their client for repeat business. Northern Rock's accounts were given a clean bill of health by its auditors, without any concerns raised about its business model. In their report into the Northern Rock debacle, Parliament's Treasury Select Committee noted "there appears to be a particular conflict of interest between the statutory role of the auditor, and the other work it may undertake for a financial institution".[4] Prem Sikka, Professor of Accounting at the University of Essex, who has spent decades studying the auditing firms, argues that because they are "dependent upon companies and their directors for income. The fee dependency impairs claims of independence".[5]

Subprime mortgages

While Northern Rock's troubles brought the looming global financial crash to the attention of the UK public, banks – especially in the US – had already begun to notice that all was not well. This wasn't the problem of an individual bank, or even a few individual banks, but a systemic problem. Subprime mortgages from the US had been traded globally. You might be thinking 'why would anyone buy subprime mortgages?' The answer is twofold, and necessitates two prior questions, 'why would any lender offer a subprime mortgage?', and firstly 'what is a subprime mortgage?'

Subprime mortgages were predominantly a US phenomenon, but a toxic one – and that toxicity went global. Subprime mortgages were so called because they were offered to customers with poor credit ratings, low incomes or little collateral. In the most extreme form some US lenders offered mortgages to people with no income, and no job or assets – 'NINJA mortgages' as they were nicknamed. And these 'ninja' mortgages lived up to their name – helping to assassinate several banks.

So why would a bank offer a subprime mortgage? Officially, the business model was this: the economy is booming and house prices are rising. If someone buys a house, even though they don't currently have enough income to justify being given a mortgage, the rising value of the home (and their likely rising income) will make it alright in the end. And from the bank's point of view the mortgage was secured against the home, so even if the mortgage holder failed to make the payments, the lender got the asset (the home). In the meantime too, the bank was raking in a tidy profit on the higher interest rates that subprime mortgages attracted.

If that seems to involve an unhealthy dollop of wishful thinking, that's because it does. The theory worked if you suspended critical thought and believed that house prices, and the economy more generally, would carry on rising indefinitely. I know what you're thinking, 'what sort of buffoon would believe that?' Well it wasn't only bankers and those understandably just desperate for their own home. In the UK, Chancellor, and later Prime Minister, Gordon Brown was proclaiming as late as 2007 that "we will never return to the old boom and bust".[6]

However, while the above forms the official explanation – the theoretical underpinning of subprime lending – the real motivation was far more prosaic: the need to securitise. Just as the Northern Rock model had relied upon feeding a constant stream of mortgages to its offshore arm Granite, so to meet the need for ready money US lenders had to be constantly expanding the market. This meant offering mortgages to groups that had previously been shut out – but this meant more and more mortgages were just, frankly, dodgy lending.

To put it in simple terms, if I have £1000 and lend half to someone who puts up their car as collateral, then I might charge

10% interest and get £550 back in a year's time. If they can't make the payments, they have to sell their car and I get the money anyway. But banks don't lend their own money, they create it. When a bank lends money it creates two accounts: a loan account and a deposit account. The loan account is the borrowers' and contains the loan, say £10,000. The deposit account has -£10,000 and as the loan is repaid so the two accounts balance up – except that with interest the deposit account will go above zero, creating a profit for the bank. A common belief is that banks make money by two simple transactions. First they invite people to deposit money with them and then lend it out, charging the borrower interest.[7] Actually the business is a little more complicated and a lot more profitable. They lend out money that does not exist! As Richard Murphy put it, "[banks] make cash out of thin air and then charge people for the privilege of using it".[8] At the time of the financial crisis, the New Economics Foundation estimated that "banks held just £1.25 in reserves for every £100 issued as credit".[9] But banks do not use this form of financial manipulation just to meet their own lending requirements, they do need cash (liquidity) – not least to pay other banks and the home-seller in the case of mortgages – hence their need to securitise assets such as mortgages.

OK, so that's why lenders created subprime mortgages – but why would anyone else buy them? Partially for the reasons set out above, the widespread collective delusion that finance capitalism had created a new world in which boom and bust had been permanently ended. But partially it was also because those buying had no idea what they were buying. Many of you will have witnessed a market trader selling a big bag of meat for a fiver. You know the sort, 'There's 10lbs of prime meat in here. I'm not asking £10. I'm not asking nine, eight or seven pounds. You'd do it for £6? Put your money away madam, I'm asking just £5 – a fiver – and I'll throw in a big juicy bone for the dog'. That in effect was how mortgage debt was bundled up as collateralised debt obligations (CDOs), and then traded around the world. There was no juicy bone, but it was a dog's dinner.

Mortgages are assets. Imagine if a bank gave you ownership of someone's mortgage: you'd receive a monthly income of several hundred pounds each month for the next 25 or 30 years for doing nothing. Banks don't get given mortgages though, they hold liquidity and transfer the cash to the seller to buy the home on your behalf. They then create your mortgage loan. You repay it with considerable interest and often will end up paying back around three times as much as you borrowed (of course to compensate for inflation over those years, but also to allow for a healthy helping of profit for the bank).

Diced and sliced among these bundled mortgages were subprime mortgages. Problems came when it began to emerge that these CDOs – and other assets – were in fact worth much less than had been paid for them. Banks found their assets were 'assets' in name only. As poor US citizens started defaulting on their mortgages, so large swathes of these assets became a lot less valuable.

With the securitised mortgage model, the lender is less focused on ensuring that the borrower is able to repay. They know they are selling the mortgage on to someone else – in exchange for immediate cash. Getting the cash is necessary, so that you can keep expanding and paying those bonuses.

But that still begs the question, how on earth did banks not realise what they were buying? Or, more to the point, why buy something when you don't know what it is? Andrew Haldane, an Executive Director at the Bank of England gives the example of a CDO product for which the documentation ran to 1,125,000,300 pages. Haldane commented, "an investor in a CDO squared[10] would need ... a PhD in mathematics under one arm and a diploma in speed reading under the other". To avoid these implausible necessities, banks relied upon credit ratings given to CDOs by credit rating agencies (CRAs). Unfortunately the CRAs were giving top AAA ratings to what turned out to be very mixed bags. The reasons do not flatter the credibility of CRAs: firstly, they did not assign any doubt to the belief that house prices and the economy would continue growing; and secondly it was the seller who paid the CRA to give the credit rating – a clear conflict of interest. After all, as we found earlier with auditors, he who pays the piper calls the tune. It is no surprise then that when two US-based academics, John Griffin and Dragon Tang, looked into the complex world of CRAs they concluded: "our findings suggest that conflicts of interest may be much more economically important than previously surmised."[11]

The Credit Crunch

The problems for Northern Rock occurred when the subprime mortgage lending crisis hit. As their business model relied so heavily on receiving funds via the money markets, they were particularly vulnerable when others became less willing to buy CDOs or lend to other banks. This stage of the crisis became known as the 'credit crunch'. As banks discovered their assets were not as valuable as thought, and as some banks started to apply for emergency funding, banks became less willing to lend to each other. They were worried that the borrowing bank might go bust and not repay the loan. And they were also worried about their own balance sheet, as assets they had bought were suddenly worth less than they thought, and so they wanted to hoard as much cash (liquidity) as possible to be able to pay their own debts and to cover for their depleted asset base. The banks' world view had been exposed as a delusion. Like an infant told that Father Christmas doesn't exist, the banks went into meltdown.

Unsure of the real status of other banks and even some of their own assets, banks took the quite logical step of not lending to each other. This left some banks highly illiquid (i.e. without ready money) whereas others were just plain insolvent – with their asset base in tatters. The only solution was to go to the central bank and beg for funds – but this just drew publicity to their plight and reinforced the fear enveloping the banking sector. Panic set in.

But how did this state of affairs arise? How were financial products traded as assets in fact dangerous liabilities? Was there no regulation, no oversight of what was going on? Partially the reason is that the finance sector that traded it these assets – often known as the shadow banking system – had grown in an unregulated environment, and was not subject to sufficient scrutiny. Politicians and regulators mostly ranged from ignorant (most) to complicit (a few) in leaving this system unregulated.

In 1955 John Kenneth Galbraith's seminal book *The Great Crash, 1929* was published. A *New York Times* reviewer wrote that it was: "Most intriguing for its depiction of the delusion that swept the culture, and the ways financiers and bankers, wishful academics and supine regulators wilfully ignored reality and in the process encouraged the epic collapse of the stock market." So were we, in the early 2000s, simply repeating the mistakes of 1929? Yes, in many ways we were, because that is the inherent logic of insufficiently regulated capitalism. In the following chapter I analyse how the "delusion that swept the culture" occurred in our era.

But before governments, regulators, media pundits and academics could conduct their post-mortem, there was a very real crisis still to be faced.

The bailout

Northern Rock was finally nationalised in February 2008, but not before the government had spent £100 million in consultants' fees to try to sell the bank to various consortia. Those fees were about equivalent to the building of 20 new schools. This was the price paid trying to avoid the nationalisation of Northern Rock, but then the floodgates opened.

On 29 September 2008, Bradford & Bingley was nationalised. Well, partly. The retail banking section (the normal part that you and I interact with) and its network of branches was transferred to Abbey National, while the remainder (its liabilities) was taken into public ownership. The Treasury gave Abbey National £4 billion to cover account holders' deposits not covered by the FSCS. This in effect was a bailout to the wealthy, who would have lost any savings beyond £35,000. A week later, £600 million was given to ING Direct which gratefully took the remainder of the UK arms of the collapsed Icelandic banks Kaupthing Singer & Friedlander and Heritable.

There is a debate that was never had as to whether the government was right spending billions of pounds of taxpayers' money bailing out the accounts of the rich. In 2012, HSBC estimated that the average person held less than a quarter of the 2008 FSCS limit (£8,401). They also found that 29% of people had no savings at all,[12] yet taxpayers' money went to cover the would-have-been losses of the very wealthy.

On 8 October 2008 a £50 billion part-nationalisation scheme was announced by government for banks in serious trouble, with a £250 billion fund to underwrite banks' debts. In addition the Bank of England made £200 billion available for short-term loans. It was a tacit acknowledgement that the problem was systemic. UK banks risked falling like dominoes. But until this point the banks that had run into trouble had not included the dominant high street banks. This was about to change.

The first major victim was the Royal Bank of Scotland (RBS) which required a public bailout in October 2008. This assistance provided to RBS consisted of a £400bn standby package, which included £40bn upfront – enough to build more than 1500 schools or 70 new hospitals.[13] The UK government eventually held 83% of the shares in the company. Sidelining UK competition law and EU mergers and acquisition regulations, Lloyds TSB and HBOS were merged to form Lloyds Banking Group and the government bought some shares to provide liquidity in January 2009. This did not resolve the problems and the government bought more shares in June and December 2009 as well – taking the public stake to 43%.

The knock-on effect was seen on the stock markets. Within a year of Northern Rock collapsing the world's stock exchanges had halved in value – as the growth miracle of the finance sector had been exposed as just another bubble. In October 2008 the Governor of the Bank of England, Mervyn King, spelt out the scale of the crisis:

> "It is difficult to exaggerate the severity and importance of those events. Not since the beginning of the First World War has our banking system been so close to collapse."[14]

Three months later, the Chancellor Alistair Darling announced he would insure UK banks against their toxic assets. The term 'toxic assets' deserves brief analysis: an asset is a thing of value, something toxic is a liability. What we had just taken national responsibility for were liabilities. The banks had privatised their profits, while the government nationalised their losses. It was perhaps the greatest achievement of the UK finance sector – even when apparently on its knees, the sector still knelt over prostrate politicians.

The bailout of the finance sector was the greatest transfer of wealth in human history. A seemingly unending stream of public money was handed over to some of the richest and most reckless individuals on the planet.

In its defence the government had to act to avert a total meltdown of the banking system. The banks hold our cash, they hold our savings, they have our mortgages, and the wider finance sector invests our pension funds. Our bills are paid by direct debits, our shopping is paid for using debit or credit cards, our wages and benefits are transferred into our accounts. The system is vital. Whatever we think of the bank bailout, doing nothing was not an option. Northern Rock's customers queued for hours precisely because they saw the risks of their bank going under.

But even under a Labour government, the option of full nationalisation was ruled out. Instead bank shareholders – warned when they bought them that shares may go up as well as down – saw the institutions saved and some value maintained. The finance sector had failed spectacularly and in doing so had brought the economy to its knees. The government had to intervene, but not necessarily in the way that it did.

What was bailed out?

If someone walks into a pub and declares their jacket to be worth £300, but everyone else declares it to be worth a mere £50 – has £250 been wiped off the economy?

That may seem like an odd question, but news reports sometimes say things like, "World stock markets tumbled sharply again on Thursday, wiping nearly £50 billion off the value of Britain's biggest listed companies". Further into the report we might learn that in fact it is worse: "and £110 billion has been wiped off in the past week"!

Whoops, that is careless! Britain's biggest companies have lost £110 billion! But it's never entirely real in the first place. Going back to the someone in the pub with his '£300 jacket'. Let's say he's a scam artist this time. He walks in and says here's my £300 jacket, and has planted a couple of his mates in the pub to talk it up, say how lovely it is (reminiscent of the Emperor's New Clothes is it not?) and fool someone, singled out as a possible target, into paying £300 for a £50 coat. If the target buys, then he will lose £250 if he tries to sell it on. That is because the asset has a true value of £50.

Back in the stock market, this fluctuation between confidence and panic would not be a problem if it was only one rogue scam artist – the problem for the stock markets is, this is the system. As the chief executive of a financial advisory business said, "A big part of the problem is that accounting rules have allowed banks to inflate the value of their assets. Accounting has become a new exercise in creative fiction with the result that banks are carrying a lot of "sludge" assets clogging up the balance sheet".[15]

It is for this reason that seemingly sensible, educated, intelligent people panic when anyone points out the Emperor's flies are undone, let alone that he is also exposing himself. So when AAA-rated CDOs (£300 jackets) are pointed out to be near junk (£50 jackets) the system seizes up in the same way that the target in the pub won't buy from the scam artist again.

On such occasions these same great brains (who never predicted this could happen) start using infantile playground language: warning against 'scaring off the confidence fairy' or 'talking down the economy' – as if a sound economy would collapse because someone says something negative. In the same way that most of us aren't reduced to gibbering wrecks because someone takes a disliking to us, sound economies don't collapse because of a few words.

Of course in 2008 economies started collapsing for the very real reason that they were based on the valuation of scam artists. Governments around the world stepped in and guaranteed much of the scam artists' nigh on worthless assets.

The question is will the government (in contrast to the target in the pub) be fooled twice and bail out again or will it learn from its mistakes and take a different course of action in future?

Hitting the rest of the economy

The near collapse of the banking sector did not just have an impact in the finance sector of the economy, it sent shockwaves reverberating around the whole economy.

As the banks refused to lend to each other, their illiquidity meant they were unable to lend to consumers and businesses too. This had an impact on consumer spending as banks refused to offer loans and mortgages as readily. The retail sector, dependent on consumer spending fed by borrowing, took a hit. As mortgage lending (and therefore home purchases) dried up, spending on furnishings and white goods for new homes also declined.

Then there was the fear factor. As people saw the banks in trouble – the government spending billions in a panic to bail them out – they became fearful for the future. As the rest of the economy started to take a hit, employers laid off staff, cut working hours and overtime, and cancelled pay rises. People who feel their future is insecure don't make big purchases. Instead they did what the banks were doing, hoarding their cash for a rainy day and not spending it in the shops. Quite rationally they started to become more cautious – they borrowed less and paid back more of their debts.

When the banks started to feel the pinch, they not only went begging for public money, but they tried to sort their balance sheets. One way to do this was to increase their profit margins: this meant they hiked interest rates for borrowing, but cut them for people's current and savings accounts – so the interest they charged you on a loan went up, while the interest on your savings went down. This gave people less money to spend in the rest of the economy. The banks also started cutting their labour costs, sacking staff in their thousands.

By now the retail sector was suffering from reduced consumer confidence and so it reacted quite logically. It cut its staff too, reducing its costs – but with the banks doing the same there were even more people out of work with less money to spend – hitting the economy overall.

As the crisis was global – hitting major UK export markets like the US and Ireland particularly hard – manufacturers were suffering too. They cut staff, and those staff that remained often had their pay or working hours cut.

As more and more people became unemployed or had their pay frozen or their hours reduced, so more people began defaulting on their mortgages and bank loans – further hitting the banks, and making them more cautious in their lending.

All of this was happening as the banking crisis was unfolding – reinforcing the problems. Finally, the government started to suffer. It received less revenue in corporation tax as the banks were making losses not profits. The rising unemployment caused by the laying off of staff meant fewer people paying taxes and more people claiming benefits. As fewer people were spending as much in the shops, VAT revenues reduced and corporation tax receipts from this sector declined too. For government, income reduced and outgoings increased.

So government then started tightening its belt – laying off staff and imposing pay freezes. This is a real false economy for government, since it already reclaims about a third of a state employee's salary through income tax and national insurance. Then it gains more through council tax and VAT when they shop. And when public sector workers are laid off then it is the government that pays redundancy packages as well as social security payments like jobseeker's allowance and housing benefit.

If the general public, private sector and government tighten their belts simultaneously, then the situation can deteriorate into a spiral of decline. We have witnessed that most dramatically in European countries like Greece and Spain, but it has also happened in the UK which recorded the longest and deepest slump since the 1870s – with the corresponding longest drop in living standards (as average wages fall below the rising cost of living) which continued six years on from the run on Northern Rock.

Quantitative Easing

A strange new phrase entered our vocabulary following the banking crisis: quantitative easing (QE). It is often referred to as 'printing money'. In fact it is more accurately described as giving banks cheap credit. QE works by the central bank, in the UK the Bank of England, buying assets – usually government bonds – using money it has simply created out of thin air. The institutions selling those bonds (the commercial banks or other finance companies) will then have new money in their accounts, which then boosts the money supply.

The policy began in January 2009 under the Labour government and was continued and extended by Cameron's coalition government. The use of QE is based on the assumption that our economic system is in crisis due to a lack of available credit (a credit crunch) and a lack of lending. When interest rates are reduced to low levels and that fails to spur businesses and people to spend and borrow (since saving is unattractive when inflation outstrips interest rates), the only remaining solution is QE.

The problem with QE was not the policy itself, but the diagnosis that prescribed it. The UK economy was not suffering from a lack of credit predominantly. It suffered from a lack of demand. Unemployment, underemployment and wage constraint had produced a situation in which living standards were falling – people inevitably reduced their spending.

Separately, the government under its austerity programme had massively cut its capital spending and slashed the welfare budget, sucking further billions out of the economy.

Government ministers like Business Secretary Vince Cable complained that the banks were not lending to small businesses yet why would they in a climate of falling demand, and wider financial uncertainty?

To make the case that QE is necessary, some pointed to statistics showing that the number of small business loans rejected by the banks has quadrupled since the crisis. This was hardly surprising since it is likely a higher proportion of business loan applications were to cover (what they hoped were temporary) shortfalls, rather than to invest. Likewise banks, whose reckless lending practices played a major role in causing the crisis, had rightly become more cautious. And of course, the same business plan in 2006/07 at a time of lower unemployment and rising wages was a lot more attractive to invest in than it was post-crash.

The far bigger problem facing the UK economy was not a lack of credit, but a lack of demand – and that required putting more money, not less, in people's pockets. It would mean doing the exact opposite of the austerity both political parties were advocating.

Meanwhile the Bank of England's QE programme grew to £325 billion. The banks clearly did not use this effective subsidy to extend credit. Instead, they used the extra liquidity to speculate in derivatives markets and to invest in safer foreign markets.

This is not to say QE is always a bad policy. It's not, but in the post-crash climate of the UK it quickly outlived its utility. Part of the problem is the limited policy options open to the outsourced (independent) Bank of England and the lack of any coherent strategy from government.

A political failure

We live in a democracy. The word 'democracy' is a portmanteau of two Greek words 'demos' (meaning 'the people') and 'kratos' (meaning 'to rule'). So 'democracy' means 'the people rule'.

We elected politicians to look after our interests. Every stage of the crash – from the run on the Rock, to the credit crunch, to the billion-pound bailout – showed how little our politicians understood the economic system that they had been lauding. But at every stage of the crash government intervention was necessary, so politicians were racing to catch up in understanding the system that was crashing before their eyes.

It may seem a little unfair to be too harsh, since this was a failure on a scale not seen before, but it was not wholly unique. In the mid-1980s the Johnson-Matthey bank needed emergency funding from the Bank of England, guaranteed by the Treasury and therefore the taxpayer. The debacle was on a small scale compared with the near meltdown faced 25 years later, but what is interesting is that the Bank of England sued the bank's auditors for damages. I asked Prem Sikka, Professor of Accounting at the University of Essex, whether any action had been taken against auditors in response to the banking failures of 2008/09. Prem told me "No UK auditor has been sued or disciplined after the 2007 banking crash". His explanation is that governments had no intention of offending the major players of their high finance driven economy.

Chief among those politicians dazzled by the world of high finance was the 'iron chancellor' Gordon Brown – at the heart of UK economic policy as Chancellor from 1997 to 2007. He described himself as an "evangelist for globalisation". In one of his final acts as Chancellor, just a few weeks before he succeeded Tony Blair as Prime Minister and just a few months before the collapse of Northern Rock, Brown addressed the City of London.

"Over the ten years that I have had the privilege of addressing you as Chancellor, I have been able year by year to record how the City of London has risen by your efforts, ingenuity and creativity to become a new world leader ... So I congratulate you Lord Mayor and the City of London on these remarkable achievements, an era that history will record as the beginning of a new golden age for the City of London."

His words appear humorous now – heralding "a new golden age" just two months before the run on Northern Rock – but they also reflected the craven belief that what was good for the finance sector was good for the UK economy.

It wasn't just under Gordon Brown, as Chancellor then Prime Minister, that the finance sector achieved such a powerful position. Though he continued and developed the great experiment, he was not its architect. The next chapter 'Sowing the seeds' looks at how the finance sector grew to become so dominant in the UK economy.

2

Sowing the seeds

Margaret Thatcher's government swept to power in 1979. It was to remake Britain in a way that no other government had done since Clement Attlee's Labour government in 1945. A senior civil servant at the time described Thatcher's new government as ushering in "a revolution" in "political and economic philosophy". As her longest serving Chancellor and chief architect of the 'great experiment', Nigel Lawson, said "our policies aimed at a conscious break ... with the entire post-war political consensus". Their plan was "to change the entire culture of a nation from anti-profits, anti-business, government-dependent lassitude and defeatism, to a pro-profit, pro-business, robustly independent vigour and optimism".[1] The rhetoric was as clear as the political ideology that informed it.

The central objectives of their 'great experiment' were to:

- cut public services and overall public spending
- privatise public assets and publicly owned industries
- privatise and deregulate the housing market
- weaken the bargaining position of workers in the labour market
- substantially reform the taxation system
- deregulate private industry, especially the finance sector

The 'great experiment' was launched following a decade punctuated by the 'oil crisis' – when the relatively underdeveloped oil producing countries not unreasonably asked the oil-consuming countries of the world (most highly developed) to pay more for their product. In the UK, the 1970s were also the pinnacle of trade union power, when membership included nearly 14 million workers and the Conservative government of Edward Heath was ousted from power after calling an election under the slogan 'Who runs Britain, the government or the unions?'. The public answered by electing a Labour government. But the global economic turmoil and the failure of pay to keep pace with inflation – predominantly caused by the rising oil price – caused more industrial unrest and workers quite understandably fought to maintain their standards of living.

These two factors – rising oil prices and rising wage demands backed by a strong trade union movement – meant that company profits were squeezed. From 1964-73 capital invested in British industry produced a return of 9.9%. In the period 1973-79 this fell to 6.5%.[2] In the 1970s, following years of gradual decline, the wealth of the richest 1% of the population was at its lowest point in the modern history of the UK, as the chart right demonstrates.

So while the 1970s was a relatively bad decade for big business and the richest 1% (they only received six times the income of the average person), it was also the culmination of an era in which the civilising forces of progressive taxation, social security, the state pension, public housing, the NHS, comprehensive education, and strong trade unions had delivered greater equality than Britain had ever seen before or since. As the graph then shows, the election of the Thatcher government in 1979 put into reverse that 80-year trend.

The chart (right) shows what happened to the top 1%, but for the least wealthy 50% the effects are even more shocking. According to the Office for National Statistics the poorest half of the UK population held 11% of the nation's wealth in 1986. Twenty years later that had fallen to just 1%.[3] The 'great experiment' managed

Share of all income received by the richest 1% in Britain

Source: Danny Dorling – Fair Play, The Policy Press, 2012

to generate an unprecedented rise in inequality – a major cause of the economic crisis that began in 2008.

While the 1970s were a period of relative equality – coming after a period of improving living standards – they were also a decade of industrial and economic turmoil. The Thatcher government was elected pledging to resolve this turbulence. Her party had identified the trade unions and the state itself as the cause of the UK's problems, and set about establishing a radically different course.

Rolling back the state: public sector cuts

The 1979 Conservative manifesto was explicit, "the State takes too much of the nation's income; its share must be steadily reduced". Once elected that commitment was put into practice – a White Paper published to coincide with the 1980 Budget proclaimed the government's aim "not merely to halt the growth of public expenditure but progressively to reduce it". Aside from the selling off of public assets, regular state spending was also to be rolled back – with education and housing budgets particularly in the firing line.

However, overall spending rose considerably under the Thatcher government. Partly, this was because unemployment tripled by the mid-1980s meaning fewer people in work paying taxes and generating revenue for government, and instead receiving benefits. In Thatcher's first three years, public spending rose by 3.5 percentage points as a proportion of GDP.

However in the mid-1980s there were significant public sector cuts. Between 1983 and 1989 public spending fell 8% relative to GDP. As a former senior cabinet minister in her government said that cutting public spending was particularly difficult "since it affects services which people have come to consider as rights"[4] – indeed, when people pay their taxes they expect good education and health systems, social security when in need, and other services. By the end of Thatcher's time in office, public spending had decreased from just over 38% of national income in 1979 to just under 36%. This may sound like a relatively small decline, but it represented a cut worth tens of billions of pounds in today's prices.

Individualism was a key part of the ideology that underpinned the 'great experiment'. By emphasising self-reliance – to the point of selfishness – misfortunes caused by circumstances beyond people's control or personal misjudgements became something to be blamed for and ashamed of. This was part of the propaganda necessary to chip away at public support for social entitlements.

"I like paying taxes. With them I buy civilisation" said the US judge Oliver Wendell Holmes, Jr. What became clear under the 'great experiment' is that when the state (bought by those taxes) is rolled back, so are its civilising effects. As well as the trebling of unemployment by the mid-1980s, crime doubled as Britain became more unequal and divided. Thatcher famously declared, in an interview with *Woman's Own*, "There is no such thing as society. There are individual men and women, and there are families". This was not merely a statement of philosophy, it was a statement of intent: 'don't expect society to help you'.

Public services also provide a vital safety net in times of recession – creating what are known as 'automatic stabilisers'. As the chart below shows, when recessions hit, public spending increases as a percentage of GDP – as more people are forced to rely on social security, and the government receives less tax revenue. The lower public spending drops, the less effective are those automatic stabilisers.

Spending as % of GDP

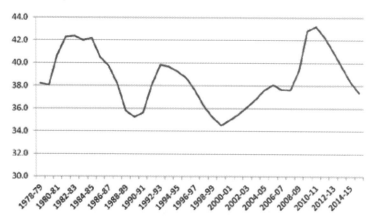

The chart above also shows that public spending as proportion of GDP was, on average, lower under the government of John Major (1990-97) than under Thatcher (1979-1990), and lower under Tony Blair's government (1997-2007) than under either Major or Thatcher. What the Thatcher government began though was a trend of falling public spending (the blips of recessions aside). Though the 2008 recession represented a particularly large blip, the intention to restore the downward trend is equally clear.

Privatisation: Selling off the family silver

The Thatcher government will forever be associated with privatisation – described as "the jewel in the crown of the government's legislation programme".[5] But far from believing it to be a jewel, former Conservative Prime Minister Harold MacMillan (1957-1963) described it as more of a heist, accusing Thatcher's government of "selling off the family silver".

The ground was prepared for Thatcher's Conservatives by the outgoing Labour government of Jim Callaghan, albeit under the direction of the International Monetary Fund (IMF). At the IMF's behest, the Callaghan government sold part of its shareholding in the then nationalised British Petroleum (later rebranded simply to BP). Writing in his diary on 24 June 1977, then cabinet minister Tony Benn noted:

> "We have handed some of the most valuable assets of this country to the Shah [of Iran], to the Americans and to private shareholders, and I am ashamed to be a member of the cabinet that has done this ... We have provided a blueprint for selling off public assets in the future and we will have no argument against it."[6]

His words were prescient. One of the first decisions of the new Thatcher government was to sell further shares in the nationally-owned company – and for the first time taking the government's shareholding below 51%. As then Financial Secretary and later Chancellor Nigel Lawson noted in his memoirs, in a sentence predicted by Benn, "[it was] a measure to which Labour could hardly object very strongly since it had already resorted to it in 1977."[7]

Nevertheless, when BP was fully privatised in the late 1980s, significant consternation was caused when the emir of Kuwait bought a significant shareholding in the company. BP was not just another privatisation. Oil made the economy go around and the Thatcher government did not want a Middle Eastern government to have sway over the UK in such a crucial area. The free market ideology of the Thatcher government butted up against the nationalism of her party. The Prime Minister, Chancellor and Foreign Secretary all met to devise a way to keep privatised BP in the hands of "one of us", as Thatcher might have said – and so a UK buyer was found. The government recognised the need for strategic control of a national asset, even as it was selling it off. This highlights a great contradiction, and pitfall, of privatisation: you can't control what you don't own.

In a 1980 lecture called 'The New Conservatism' Lawson made the extraordinary claim that "governments cannot create economic growth". Ironically, by foregoing many of the levers that enabled governments to do just that, Lawson had limited its ability to do so. But what he was really saying is that it was not the role of government to create growth – and neither, in his opinion, was it the role of the government to manage any trading part of the economy:

> "By the 1992 general election, about two thirds of the formerly State-owned industries in the UK had been transferred to the private sector. Some forty-six major businesses, employing some 900,000 people, had been privatised."

This statement was made prior to the privatisation of the railways under John Major, the part-privatisation of air traffic control under New Labour or the privatisation of Royal Mail under David Cameron's Conservative-led coalition. The list of what was privatised through the 1980s is colossal: British Petroleum, British Telecommunications, British Gas, Enterprise

Oil, the regional electricity boards, the national grid, Cable & Wireless, British Aerospace, Britoil, Amersham International, Fairey Engineering, Ferranti, National Freight, International Aeradio, British Rail Hotels, Girobank, the British National Oil Corporation (setup to explore for, extract, refine and distribute North Sea Oil), the regional water authorities, British Airways, and hundreds of thousands of council homes.

It is worth noting the language used by MacMillan, Benn and Lawson in the quotes above. What was sold off is variably described as silver, assets, industries and businesses – all of which conveys value. Many of these valuable assets and businesses provided income for the state.

As Labour MP John McDonnell said, privatisation is "slaughtering geese that lay golden eggs, for a one-day fry-up".[8] Successive governments have sold off public assets that were built up and maintained by taxpayers, and that also created revenue for us as well. This was selling what was collectively ours as a nation. As privatisation architect and former chancellor Nigel Lawson confesses, "in advance of every significant privatisation, public opinion was invariably hostile to the idea".[9]

If there was hostility in advance, it was often only increased when it was found that in order to privatise, profitable operations within businesses were often separated from the unprofitable parts (which stayed with the taxpayer). Likewise any debts that the state businesses held were often taken on by the taxpayer prior to privatisation, so as not to deter private buyers. As we saw with the banks in Chapter 1, the state nationalised the losses and privatised the profits. One example was the privatisation of water, where the environmental management of rivers and waterways remained with the state. As Nigel Lawson casually states, "once it was clear the regulatory and environmental responsibilities would remain in the public sector, privatisation never looked seriously at risk".[10]

An opinion poll in 1989 found that 79% of the UK population was opposed to water privatisation. In 2006, a Populus poll for the BBC *Daily Politics* programme found 56% still believed that water should be in public ownership.[11] In 2013 the Class thinktank found that 68% of people wanted the energy companies renationalised, 66% wanted the railways back in public ownership, and 67% favoured the recently privatised Royal Mail being run in the public sector.[12]

The Thatcher government emphasised that these privatisations were spreading share ownership – creating a 'popular capitalism', as they tried to coin it. But people were really only buying themselves out – paying to get a small proportion of what they already collectively owned. By the end of eighteen years of Conservative rule, UK individuals owned 16.5% of UK company shares. In 1975, individuals had held 37.5%. Indeed far from the Thatcher era being a revolution in popular share ownership, her privatising government saw foreign ownership of UK company shares more than treble – a trend that continued under her successors, as the foreign ownership of UK shares went from 3.6% of the total in 1981 to well over 40% thirty years later.[13]

Taxpayers were further robbed by the downgrading of the state earnings-related pension scheme (SERPS). The scheme was established in 1978 by Labour minister Barbara Castle in the government of Jim Callaghan. It provided workers an extra pension worth about 25% of their earnings. If you worked for an employer that provided an occupational final salary pension scheme then you could opt out of SERPS. When the Thatcher government reduced the value of SERPS to 20% of earnings in 1986, it also allowed individuals to opt out of SERPS into personal pension schemes. This was promoted as giving people choice to opt out of employers' schemes and choose their own – and helped establish a new and now largely discredited market for private pensions. About 1 in 7 workers did opt out into personal pensions in the first year, and this rose to over 1 in 4 by 1993. However, as pensions scandals mounted and the inefficiency of many schemes became clear this reduced dramatically so that by 2005 fewer than 1 in 10 workers opted into personal pension schemes.[14] As pensions expert Bryn Davies told me, "Given the extent of mis-selling there is no clear evidence that anyone ended up being better-off by having a personal pension, rather than remaining in SERPS. The substantial subsidies given to encourage Additional Private Pensions ended up with the providers, rather than the individual savers."[15] The private pensions industry continues to receive huge tax reliefs, yet delivers relatively poor value for money for pensioners. In 2008, private pensions (occupational and personal) paid out £35 billion to pensioners, yet that same year the private pensions industry received £37.6 billion in tax reliefs.[16]

Achieving value for money was at best a secondary consideration for the Thatcher administration. The attitude of the Thatcher government was driven by ideology, summed up by her longest reigning chancellor Nigel Lawson, when he said, "I believed that it was important to privatise as much as possible as quickly as possible".[17] Their aim was to expose more and more of the nation's natural monopolies to what former Labour prime minister, and great nationaliser, Clement Attlee referred to as "wasteful competition".

We don't believe that doctors, nurses, firefighters or librarians need to be motivated by bonuses or market competition. So why should people providing homes with water, electricity or gas not also be motivated by a sense of public good – are they any more inherently selfish than someone working in a library? The issue is not predominantly one of personal motivation or morality, but of institutional form. Whatever your motives to serve the public or do good, the structure of working in a private company will mean that your work has been structured to fulfil the primary legal duty to maximise shareholder profit.

The structural need to make profit also changes the nature of a service. When bus companies were privatised and minimum service requirements removed or diluted, the new bus companies dropped unprofitable routes that had previously been cross-subsidised by the more profitable routes, because the primary aim was no longer to provide a service, but to make a profit. While economic efficiency matters, public transport also fulfils a social need. Imagine how gridlocked city centres would be without the network of public transport to ferry people in and out efficiently, leaving transport to the free market – individuals driving cars in and out – would be a disaster, not just logistically and economically, but environmentally too. So there are important social, economic and environmental reasons why public transport exists.

To a lesser extent, health was also placed on the altar of private profit as the Thatcher government was also responsible for the privatisation of hospital cleaning services. To drive down costs, contractors cut staff so that the number of hospital cleaners halved between 1983 and 2009. Unsurprisingly, the number of hospital acquired infections rose as a result, costing money in litigation and compensation, and more tragically in lost lives.

But the Thatcher government was not satisfied with just the privatisation of UK industry and services, it lobbied hard for liberalisation and privatisation abroad as well – and nowhere more so than in the European Community (EC), now the European Union (EU). Ironically as EC directives were imposed to promote privatisation many other European nations dragged their heels, while their state-owned companies bought lucrative shares in the UK's privatised utilities. Despite her later euroscepticism and patriotism, Thatcher's legacy is the selling off of UK national assets to European companies, many of which were state-owned.

Cooking the books: privatising the Treasury

Labour increased public sector spending substantially in their period in office (1997-2010) – including average annual increases in NHS spending of over 7% in real terms, which took UK health spending from 6% of GDP in 2000 to 9% in 2010[18] and closer to the average spent by other developed nations on healthcare. However, just as Jim Callaghan's government had provided the blueprint for that of Thatcher, so John Major had provided the blueprint for Blair and Brown as much of this extra investment was funnelled through the private finance initiative (PFI). While the Major government signed 21 PFI deals, by the end of Blair's term as Prime Minister in 2007 850 had been signed.

PFI worked by giving the finance sector the opportunity to fund public sector projects and then charge public bodies for the repayments and maintenance contracts. In 2011, there was around £300 billion of debt owed by public bodies to PFI companies. And what has this £300 billion of debt brought us? New public assets valued at just over £50 billion. New Labour had effectively handed over public investment to the scam artist in the pub that we met in chapter 1.

While this sounds like an irredeemably bad bit of government procurement, the advocates of PFI argue that because the finance is delivered by the private sector the risks involved are transferred too. Another professed advantage is that the cost of the project goes to the public body involved, rather than the Treasury, so it is off the public sector balance sheet – which means it does not count towards the government debt total.

Sadly the reality is that the PFI proponents had been overcome by a modern-day alchemy delusion (in the middle ages it was a common theory that base metal could be transformed into gold). All that glistens is not gold and while the case for PFI was superficially attractive, the logic gap was always clear.

Two high profile examples demonstrate why the advocates of PFI were delusional. The London Underground public-private partnership (PPP) was the largest PFI deal in history – worth £30 billion over 30 years. But although only signed in 2003 it began to collapse in 2007 when one of the consortia which had won the contract to modernise the London Underground's infrastructure went into administration.

The failure of one half of the PPP deal resulted in London Underground having to bail out Metronet's debts in February 2008 with a £1.7 billion grant from the Department for Transport (DfT). London Underground was formerly directly funded by the DfT, but on handing control to the London Mayor, the Treasury insisted that the private sector would be more efficient at delivering major infrastructure upgrades and maintenance and so privatised it, before handing it over to the Mayor's Transport for London (TfL) authority, which runs the tube network on a day-to-day basis.

But Metronet only managed half the PPP, the other half was run by another private consortia called Tube Lines. With their contract over cost and behind schedule they were finally bought out by TfL in 2010 – bringing to a calamitous end one of the largest privatisation debacles in history.

The House of Commons Transport select committee (TSC) investigated the failure of the contracts and concluded:

> "Some 20 months following the demise ... the Government is no nearer being able to demonstrate that the PPP provides value for money for the taxpayer."

The TSC report followed earlier damning reports on the PFI by the National Audit Office, the House of Commons' Public Accounts Committee and House of Lords' Economic Affairs Committee. The government never will demonstrate that PFI provides value for money for one very simple reason: it doesn't.

In fact far from providing value for money, PFI saddles the public sector with massive liabilities. In the case of the London Underground PPP the consortia involved could not meet the seemingly lucrative contracts they had signed and had their debts bailed out with public money. The mantra of privatisation again: the profits shall be privatised, the losses shall be nationalised. Far from being transferred, risk had been increased and then handed back.

In south-east London, the closure of most front line services at Lewisham hospital were approved. Lewisham was a successful hospital serving its local community, but services in the wider area had to be slashed as a result of the bankruptcy of the neighbouring South London Healthcare Trust – brought down by the unaffordable costs of two PFI hospitals – but Lewisham bore the brunt. PFI was rescued at the expense of patient care. A rearguard action by the local community significantly ameliorated the proposed cuts to their hospital.

By loading public bodies with debts, public spending was also reduced as more NHS, schools, and transport spending actually was spent on repaying the overpriced debts they had been lumbered with through PFI.

By privatising more and more of UK industry, the state had debilitated its ability to stimulate the economy in times of recession or to invest for social need, rather than for short-term profit. A powerful economic lever had been lost.

Privatising and deregulating the housing market

Housing merits some particular analysis within the overall story of privatisation, as it was the credit-led housing boom that played a large part in the early 1990s recession, and the deregulation and trading of mortgage debt that was integral to the 2008 crash too.

Over 1.7 million council homes were sold under right-to-buy between 1979 and 1992. Thatcher's great aim was to increase home ownership, and for many years that happened. Ironically though, by selling off council housing and not replacing it, her reforms inflated house prices and prepared the conditions in which home ownership became unaffordable for more and more of the population. The gross inequality that now exists means an increasing section of the population simply cannot afford home ownership. In 2012, for the first time since the second world war, home ownership levels in the UK declined. And far from right-to-buy leading to greater home ownership, an investigation in 2013 found one-third of the council homes sold in the 1980s were now owned by private landlords. Among those landlords was Charles Gow, the son of Thatcher's housing minister Ian Gow, who owned 40 ex-council homes.[19] Of course, many people who bought their own council houses at large discounts benefited from the plan either by cashing out or from the added collateral and borrowing power. But right-to-buy had caused a shortage of council housing for those who needed it, and placed public housing in the hands of profiteers.

In 1989 the Thatcher government removed rent controls. From 1988 to 1993 Conservative governments also gave tax reliefs to providers of private rental accommodation – under the 'Business Expansion Scheme'. These two moves – generous tax incentives and the opportunity to charge ever higher rents – unsurprisingly increased the size of the private rental market, and average rental costs.

Landlords play a parasitic role in the housing market. They live from the work of others whether directly through the payment of rent by working tenants or through the receipt of housing benefit (paid for by taxation) for low income households. This parasitical relationship plays a major role in deepening inequality, as wealthy landlords suck income from their tenants and use this income to buy further properties and further inflate housing prices – pushing home ownership further from the reach of the sucked-dry housing underclass. The expansion in the proportion of households renting privately, doubling in the past twenty years while social rents have halved in the last thirty-five years, shows how housing rentals are no longer predominantly paid to government to fund housing policy, but to private landlords to build personal wealth. It is the story of the UK economy in microcosm.

Between 1979 and 2013, UK house prices doubled in real terms (adjusted for inflation). A house you might consider buying today for £200,000 would only have cost you half as much in 1979[20] – yet the building is older and, even if only marginally, nearer the end of its useful life. Although reliable data is harder to come by, rental costs have increased similarly. Even in the years following the crash, the average UK rent increased by 11.5% in real terms between 2009 and 2012.[21]

More of our income being spent on housing costs means less money being spent in the job creating parts of the economy. And it also means more of our incomes being paid in mortgage interest to banks, and in rents to landlords, exacerbating inequality.

Housing has been a major cause of widening inequality in the UK – shifting income from the poorer into wealth for the rich. The land is there already, and mostly the housing is too, yet we have all been paying more because the wealthy have come to treat housing as another speculative investment.

Weakening workers

A central part of the great experiment was to weaken labour – not the political party, but the people who gave the party its name. Thatcher's government saw it as their role to take the force out of the labour force.

Looking across the Atlantic, Thatcher's Chancellor lauded the crushing of labour power in the US:

> "over the past ten years, the workers of western Europe have seen their real earnings rise by around an eighth; over the same period their American counterparts have been prepared to accept a small reduction in real earnings".[22]

US workers had of course 'accepted' no such thing. It had been forced upon them through often long and crushing labour disputes with union-busting management.

The strength of UK trade unions had increased in the 1970s, when several significant industrial disputes led to victories in favour of workers (resulting in the one-eighth pay increase Lawson regrets). For the Thatcher government "a reduction in union power was an important aim of Conservative policy even though it was couched in language of checking abuse, democratising procedures, and so on".[23] In other words the bluster about 'too powerful unions, led by undemocratic union barons' was just a cover for the real agenda of curtailing the power of workers to organise in their own interests and achieve fair pay and working conditions. The same slanders remain in use today to undermine the democratic decisions of workers and their democratically elected union leaders.

By 1984, the Thatcher government had banned the 'closed shop' (workplace or industry agreements that required workers to hold union membership), outlawed secondary industrial action (groups of workers taking strike action in solidarity with other workers), flying pickets (supporters of a strike action picketing workplaces) and required postal balloting before strike action (union members could no longer vote to strike on a show of hands at a meeting). The decline of unionised workplaces, and the legal restrictions placed on trade unions meant that the proportion of workers covered by collective bargaining agreements declined from 85% when Thatcher's government took office to fewer than 40% today.

Between 1945 and 1978 UK unemployment had never risen above one million, yet since that time it has never been below 1.5 million. The major part of the reason for that is what the Thatcher government described as "the abandonment of the unfulfillable commitment to full employment, which had enabled the unions to hold previous governments to ransom".[24] Just as government had abdicated any responsibility to steer the economy, it also no longer saw for itself any role in guaranteeing employment for its citizens, something to which the governments of the previous thirty five years had been committed (and with some success). Subsequently, unemployment has been higher in every year since.

Having a large number of unemployed workers also serves to weaken the wage bargaining of those in work – employers (and employees) know that replacements for existing workers are available. Conversely, under conditions of (near) full employment, employers need to reward workers to retain them, as they cannot so easily find replacements. Thatcher's government appeared indifferent to the misery of mass unemployment, which rose for seven straight years following her election in 1979, peaking at over three million in the middle of 1986. The rationale then was the same as Prime Minister David Cameron's aide Lord Young explained in 2013, "labour can be cheaper and higher quality, meaning that return on investment can be greater".[25] In short, unemployment is a good thing for corporate profits. For a lower amount of investment (in wages), the same work could be done – meaning higher profits for the employers. Lower wages and higher profits produce widening inequality. It was not just unions that were under attack, but whole sectors of the economy where labour power was strong, like mining and manufacturing, that were also targeted. The manufacturing industry – a bastion of unionised labour was devastated with two million jobs lost in the 1980s.

It is no surprise that the percentage of national wealth going to workers in wages has declined from nearly 65% of GDP in the mid-1970s to 55% by 2010. Where did this wealth go? Over the same period, the rate of corporate profit has increased from 13% to 21%.[26] In his memoirs, Nigel Lawson praises himself for "the creation of a climate in which profitability improved dramatically".[27] This was the redistribution of wealth from workers to employers, from labour to capital.

Wage councils were also dismantled in this period. They had existed in a number of industries to agree minimum wage levels (long before the Labour government introduced the national minimum wage in 1998). Under Thatcher wage councils had their powers severely constrained and some were abolished. Under John Major's government, the 1993 Trade Union Reform and Employment Rights Act abolished all but one of the remaining 26 wage councils, at a stroke removing the remaining minimum wage protection for 2.5 million low paid workers. The one survivor of the assault on wage councils was the agricultural wages board, which survived until abolition by David Cameron's government in 2013.

Although heralded as one of the Labour government's finest achievements, the national minimum wage (NMW) was set at a very low level – introduced in 1998 at just £3.60 per hour and only for workers aged 22 or over. Although the NMW increased above the level of inflation in its early years, since the financial crisis the NMW was cut by 7% in real terms between 2008 and 2013.[28]

By weakening workers' bargaining power and their pay, profitability increased from its 1970s lows. This however was never going to be sustainable in the long term (leaving aside whether such a reduction could even temporarily be desirable).

Less of our national income going to the mass of workers, reduces consumer demand and increases the prospects of workers defaulting on loans and mortgages. Driving down living standards is bad for business in the long term – even though it is good for business profits in the short term. To avoid this spiral of decline, state intervention and trade unions are needed. Thatcher's 'great experiment' eroded both.

Reform of taxation: ending redistributive taxation

Most people understand the UK taxation system to be redistributive with the richest paying proportionately more than the poorest, described by the maxim 'from each according to his ability, to each according to his needs'. But this is not the case. The tax that most people will be familiar with is income tax, which is progressive, meaning the more you earn the more you pay not just in cash amounts but as a proportion too. However this is not true for many other taxes that are levied at a flat rate on consumption e.g. VAT, and so-called 'sin taxes' on petrol, tobacco and alcohol (the latter three of which were all increased at twice the rate of inflation in the 1981 Budget, and have since been regularly uprated above inflation).

This did not happen by accident "the centrepiece of the [Thatcher government's first] Budget had to be a massive switch from direct to indirect taxes".[29] So VAT rose from 8% and 12.5% (there were two rates for different goods) to a single rate of 15%. In 1984, chancellor Nigel Lawson extended the range of goods to which VAT applied, and in 1991 the VAT rate rose again, to 17.5% – a further regressive measure that increased inequality. In 2010, the Conservative-led coalition government raised VAT even further to 20%.

The 1991 rise in VAT (from 15% to 17.5%) was a direct response to the budget shortfall caused by the hasty u-turn the government had been forced into over the Poll Tax. The Poll Tax was a fundamental shift from the rates system, a local tax administered by councils (today simply known as the council tax). Whereas the previous rates system was levied per household, the poll tax was levied on individuals – almost regardless of circumstances. While this was seen as unfair by millions, for the Thatcher government its flat rate was seen as a virtue. Government minister Nicholas Ridley MP airily declared "A duke would pay the same as a dustman". After a sustained campaign of non-payment by pensioners, students and low paid workers, the Poll Tax was scrapped and Thatcher bundled from office by her own party. The tax put huge pressure on the finances of low income households – and was a step too far by the Thatcher administration in shifting tax burden from rich to poor. But the revenue shortfall meant that taxation had to be raised elsewhere – and so VAT was raised, leaving the less well-off to disproportionately bear the burden again.

Early on, the Thatcher government cut the highest rate of income tax from 83% to 60%. As the then Financial Secretary Nigel Lawson recounts, "the cut in the top rate of income tax was massive".[30] And if that tax cut was massive, it was about to become gargantuan. In 1988 the top rate of tax declined further, from 60% to 40%. Other taxes on personal wealth were removed too including, in 1984, the investment income surcharge. Over the same period the basic rate of income tax fell only from 33% to 25%.

Very high earners got a large tax break, while anyone who bought goods in the shops had to pay a higher price. This group not only includes lower earners, but those on disability benefits, pensioners, students, and increased legions of unemployed people too. This was by no means a tax-cutting government. As the then Financial Secretary confessed at a talk in Zurich in 1981 "we have so far, on balance, increased the real burden of taxation overall".[31] To be more specific it was a government that switched from progressive taxation to largely regressive taxation (that reinforced rather than tackled inequality).

The rationale for this move was explained by Nigel Lawson in his 1988 Budget speech, "excessive rates of income tax destroy enterprise, encourage avoidance, and drive talent to more hospitable shores overseas".[32] This is the age-old belief that without incentives, and the freedom to amass unlimited wealth, rich people won't work to the best of their abilities. The other side of this equation is that poor people have to work to survive so need no incentivisation.

This rebalancing of the tax system was described in *The Guardian* as "the final disappearance of the last vestiges of the post-war consensus ... Fairness and social justice, as registered through the tax system, have ceased even to be the pretended aspiration of the Conservative Party". Elected with a landslide majority in 1997, the incoming New Labour government accommodated to this new consensus, pledging to increase neither the basic nor top rates of income tax.

Over this same period the welfare state was significantly devalued. Whereas in 1967, unemployment benefit had been worth 28% of average earnings, by the time Mrs Thatcher had been expelled from office it was only worth 18%. In 2013, Jobseeker's Allowance, as it is now known, is worth only 13% of average earnings. The same is also true of the basic state pension, which was worth 26% of average earnings in 1980, but by 2008 was worth less than 16%.[33]

The devaluation of social security benefits has been predominantly caused by breaking the earnings link in 1980, which had meant benefits rose in line with average wages. From then on, benefits only rose in line with inflation, and lost pace with average incomes. It is sobering to think that the unemployed today would be nearly 40% better off in the final year of Mrs Thatcher's reign. Other benefits have lost value too as they have been frozen or had increases capped for several years. A good example of this is Child Benefit which was frozen for the last four years of the Thatcher government and again in the first three years of the Cameron government. In the latter case that three year freeze meant a family with two children were £235 worse off in 2013. This may strike the reader as surprising given the media hysteria about rising welfare costs – but the rising welfare bill is mostly due to more pensions being paid to an ageing population, higher housing benefit costs (due to rent inflation), and greater eligibility to tax credits and other benefits due to lower wages. Indeed, the rise in welfare spending masks the declining generosity of many benefits.

But it is not just the decline in the value of benefits which is significant. It has been accompanied by a concerted propaganda campaign to demonise those in receipt of them. This began with Norman Tebbit – a minister in the Thatcher government that trebled unemployment – declaring in response to the 1981 riots, "I grew up in the '30s with an unemployed father. He didn't riot. He got on his bike and looked for work, and he kept looking till he found it". Of course the vast majority of the unemployed, then and now, are looking for work – few are rioting – but they continue to be demonised for not finding work that doesn't exist. Twenty-nine years later, Tebbit's words would be echoed by Cameron government minister Iain Duncan Smith, who said of the unemployed in former mining community Merthyr Tydfil, "[they] didn't know that if they got on a bus for an hour's journey, they'd be in Cardiff and could look for the jobs there". The problem was that when unemployed of Merthyr disembarked in Cardiff, they would find that there were already nine unemployed people for every job vacancy in that city.

But the attack on the poorest people has not only been verbal, but economic too. The tables below demonstrate that what different groups in society pay in tax has changed considerably over time:

Tax paid as % of gross income

1979 (year Thatcher government came to power)

	Poorest 10%	Middle 10%	Richest 10%
Direct taxation	14	20	23
Indirect taxation	21	18	14
Total taxation	**35**	**38**	**37**

1990 (year Thatcher left office, replaced by Major)

	Poorest 10%	Middle 10%	Richest 10%
Direct taxation	20	18	22
Indirect taxation	27	19	10
Total taxation	**47**	**37**	**32**

1997 (year Major left office, Blair came to power)

	Poorest 10%	Middle 10%	Richest 10%
Direct taxation	12	17	23
Indirect taxation	32	19	11
Total taxation	**44**	**36**	**34**

2010 (year Labour left office, Cameron came to power)

	Poorest 10%	Middle 10%	Richest 10%
Direct taxation	12	16	25
Indirect taxation	31	15	8
Total taxation	43	31	33

Source: Office for National Statistics

What these tables show is a significant shift in taxation from direct to indirect taxation, but more significantly a substantial shift of the tax burden from the richest to the poorest. This shift primarily took place during the Thatcher years, but has been largely maintained by her successors: Major, Blair and Brown.

But it wasn't just the taxation of individuals that concerned the government, taxation was cut for corporations, small businesses and on capital gains (profits made through investments). In the eighteen years of Conservative government from 1979 to 1997 corporation tax was cut from 52% to 33%. As Nigel Lawson said, "the burden needed to be shifted from companies ... to individuals".[34]

One might have expected a Labour government to have gone at least some way to reversing a rate that meant in the mid-1990s the UK had the lowest rate of corporation tax in the European Community (now the European Union). Instead the Labour government continued this downward trajectory, cutting corporation tax from 33% to 28%. The New Labour years alone meant that corporations were given tax cuts estimated to have cost the public finances over £50 billion.[35] Furthermore, under Gordon Brown, Labour cut the rate of capital gains tax on business assets from 40% to 10%.

Even though Labour left office with an even further reduced corporation tax rate, the incoming chancellor was not to be outdone. George Osborne in his 2012 Budget reduced corporation tax to 24% and announced that "by 2014, Britain will have a 22% rate of corporation tax ... And a rate that puts our country within sight of a 20% rate of business tax". He boldly stated just how low this was, at 24%: "A headline rate that is not just lower than our competitors, but dramatically lower. 18% lower than the US. 16% lower than Japan. 12% below France and 8% below Germany. An advertisement for investment and jobs in Britain".[36] It echoed the words of his predecessor, Lawson, who declared that by 1986-7, UK corporation tax was lower "than in almost any other competitor, including Japan".[37]

According to the fairytale told, "higher profits after tax will encourage and reward enterprise, stimulate innovation in all its forms, and create more jobs".[38] The reality is that by cutting taxes on the richest and weakening workers' bargaining power, the stunning effect of the Thatcher years was a near fivefold increase in corporate profitability,[39] at the expense of workers' wages and government revenue. The US, Japan, France and Germany, despite their higher rates of corporation tax, all have functioning economies and successful businesses – in many ways better and more stable than our own. The aim of this different strategy was unusually made explicit by Francis Maude, a cabinet minister in Cameron's government, who said it was "a compliment" for the UK to be described as a tax haven, and added "that is exactly what we are trying to do".[40] There was an implicit cross-party consensus, as chancellor Gordon Brown had hinted at that aim in 2006 addressing the City of London where he pledged his allegiance to "seeking a low tax economy".[41]

The rate of corporate profitability in the UK was also aided by the ending or loosening of many restrictions on capital investment opening up a financially rewarding but socially useless, and at times economically and socially harmful, finance sector – as we shall see in the next section.

But it is first worth considering the cultural change brought about by the Thatcher government's tax changes. The Thatcher government's justification for cutting tax, was partially because with lower rates, "taxpayers will be less inclined to pay expensive accountants to devise complex schemes to reduce their liability"[42] – inadvertently revealing in whose interests they served: who else but the rich can afford "expensive accountants" anyway?

When the 2010 the coalition government was formed, 23 of the 29 cabinet ministers were millionaires. Barely 1.5% of the UK's households are millionaires, yet in the coalition government's cabinet it was 79% – government of the rich, by the rich, for the rich. And it was no surprise when the same arguments were wheeled out again in favour of cutting taxes on the rich elite: HM Treasury commented when assessing the first year that an additional 50% rate of tax was levied in 2010-11, and up to £18 billion in pay was brought forward to avoid tax, "this behavioural response is entirely legitimate, and difficult to prevent". HM Revenue and Customs (HMRC) is it seems relaxed about avoidance and regularly makes tax deals with serial avoiders – both individuals and large corporations. Campaigning organisations such as the academic Tax Justice Network or the direct action UK Uncut, as well as the PCS union that represents workers in HMRC have brought these cosy relationships to public attention. The culture they fight against is one set by the Thatcher government: that "taxes are for the little people" as the US businesswoman and tax dodger Leona Helmsley once said, and today it seems the role of government is to support the rich to make more money. The accountant and co-founder of the Tax Justice Network, Richard Murphy, estimates that the UK has a tax gap of over £120 billion – comprising of taxes, mainly from wealthy individuals and big business, that are evaded, avoided or simply not collected. So even with reduced rates of taxation, the most powerful still avoid paying their taxes, an option not open to the tens of millions of workers whose taxes are deducted at source through PAYE, and who anyway couldn't afford the fancy accountants that enable the rich to dodge tax.

From being a driver of equality, the UK tax system is one of the key structural drivers of inequality – redistributing from poor to rich (even when the rich pay their taxes).

Deregulation of the finance sector

The finance sector has been a large and influential part of the UK economy for centuries. The industrial revolution propelled our country into becoming the dominant global power. Britain's vast empire led to investment in developing trading routes, infrastructure and industry in foreign lands to exploit their mineral wealth and people. Investment abroad required an international finance network, and this grew massively. Its legacy remains with us today: the Hong Kong Shanghai Banking Corporation – now more commonly known as HSBC – was established in 1865 to facilitate trade between Hong Kong and Europe.

HSBC is not the only legacy. The UK's offshore network of crown dependencies – from the local (Jersey, Guernsey, Isle of Man) to the exotic (Cayman Islands, British Virgin Islands, Bermuda) – are a direct legacy of empire. These minor outposts have found a niche as tax havens, enabling the super-rich and multinational companies to dodge their tax responsibilities and defraud people and governments around the world of many billions in revenue. According to tax haven experts, the crown dependencies off the coast of the UK alone could facilitate around $30 billion of tax evasion every year.[43]

While the large UK banking sector and institutionalised tax evasion and avoidance are therefore not recent phenomena, the 'great experiment' enabled the finance sector to play an increasingly dominant role in the UK economy.

The Thatcher revolution began immediately with the abolition of exchange controls in the 1979 emergency budget. Exchange controls are government-imposed limits on trading in a national currency and can help stop damaging speculative trade which causes disruption to the economy. It is no underestimation to state that removing exchange controls was an immediate disaster for the government. Money flooded out rather than in, interest rates rose, investment sagged and contributed to the sharply rising unemployment.

It was described as freeing "the pent-up demand for overseas portfolio investment".[44] In other words with restrictions removed, investors no longer scoured for good UK investments, but sought out the highest possible return on their investments anywhere in the world. UK investors bought up property and business investment opportunities abroad while investment in the UK was depressed.

What Thatcher's Conservative government did, was in contrast to the previous Conservative government led by Edward Heath (1970-74), which in 1972 greatly reduced the territories covered by the sterling area (countries between which UK currency could be freely moved). Heath was concerned that the UK's Caribbean territories (tax havens like the Cayman Islands) were a destabilising risk and in 1972 introduced exchange controls to reduce risk and protect tax revenues. The Conservative government under Thatcher was blasé about such risks, removing the controls entirely just seven years later. In doing so, Thatcher's Conservatives had abandoned the post-war consensus, a revolution in the country for sure, but also within their own party.

At the same time Thatcher's government was allowing the super-rich to keep more and more of their wealth, and rowing back from any responsibility the government once had to channel investment to create jobs and build the necessary infrastructure for people, and indeed domestic businesses, to flourish. The UK economy, under severe shock treatment, slipped into recession in 1981 as both government and business investment dipped.

Lord Lever, speaking in the House of Lords debate on the abolition of exchange controls, was unwittingly more prescient than he imagined, describing it as "a considerable encouragement to a great trading, insurance and banking nation like our own"[45] – the cultivation of this sector was to bear a very bitter fruit in 2008, and plenty of destabilisation along the way.

Removing exchange controls and allowing the value of the pound to float freely in the money markets came at a price. Market fluctuations undermined the stability that monetarists like Thatcher's chancellors Geoffrey Howe and Nigel Lawson craved. It was the latter that assertively made the case for the UK joining the European exchange rate mechanism (ERM) so that the value of the pound would be effectively pegged to that of other currencies. Leaving exchange rates to the markets meant, as then Chancellor Nigel Lawson lamented in 1987, "the absence of players who take a longer view and so provide a stabilising influence"[46] – something his successor Norman Lamont felt keenly when the UK exited the ERM on 16 September 1992 – a date that became known as 'Black Wednesday'. While currency speculators like billionaire George Soros could make considerable profits from such activities, the impact on internationally trading UK manufacturing businesses was to create the headache of coping with sometimes wildly shifting global currency prices, that could make devastating impacts on the profit margins of importing components or exporting finished goods.

Nigel Lawson, a junior Treasury minister when exchange controls were lifted and later chancellor, was a keen advocate of the European exchange rate mechanism, as a deeply flawed attempt to stabilise the exchange rate. As he reflected after leaving the Treasury:

"In a twenty-four-hour global marketplace where capital flows, often of a speculative nature, rather than trade flows, dominate, the world's experience of freely floating exchange rates has not been a happy one."[47]

Banking interests were foremost in the minds of the ideologues in the Thatcher government. While the US under Ronald Reagan was seen as an ideological counterpart of the ruling Thatcher administration, Reagan went nowhere near as far as the UK in deregulating the finance sector.

Throughout Reagan's period of office the Glass-Steagall Act was maintained. It separated retail banking (the transactions that you and I do in the high street or increasingly online) and investment banking (the speculative high risk trades that can crash economies). And as the UK government further deregulated what banks could do, the US government introduced a requirement on its banks to hold a given level of reserves (the German central bank put similar obligations on German banks). Such a policy was rejected in the UK by Thatcher's first chancellor Geoffrey Howe (and all of his successors) as it was judged that this would effectively be a tax on the banks and curtail lending. In fact, even more recklessly, in 1981 the Thatcher government under Howe's chancellorship removed the 'Reserve Assets Ratio requirement' which had meant banks had to hold at least 12.5% of their deposits as liquid assets. Had such a regulation remained in place it would have been unlikely that banks like HBOS would have gone bust nearly thirty years later. It was almost as if the finance sector was seen as an end in itself, rather than something to be regulated to ensure it could assist a stable economy.

Amazingly, the UK banking sector had no specific statutory regulation prior to the 1979 Banking Act, enacted by Jim Callaghan's outgoing Labour government. Before then the Bank of England had only informal authority over privately-owned banks, and depositors had very little protection. The guidelines governing building society lending were abolished in 1979 and the 'corset' (regulations to limit bank lending) was abolished in 1980. To facilitate further lending to consumers the restrictions on hire-purchase arrangements were lifted in 1982. These early acts allowed the finance sector to lend aggressively and would in time result in the UK becoming the most indebted nation in the western world – in terms of both personal and corporate debt. As Nigel Lawson reflects, there was a "consequent explosion of lending, and of spending financed by lending",[48] which wasn't sustainable.

In 1986 the government allowed for building societies to convert into banks with one-off share bonanzas for building society members. This resulted in the phenomenon of carpet-bagging; people opening up accounts at building societies in order to vote for conversion into banks and benefit from receipt of shares. Northern Rock transformed from building society to bank in just this way in 1997.

As the shackles came off the banking sector, by 1987 even the Thatcher government realised that the regulatory framework had to be strengthened. Even then though, in the wake of the collapse of the Johnson-Matthey Bank in 1984 (which like Northern Rocks had its accounts signed off by its auditors), bank auditors were under no obligation to share information with the regulator, the Bank of England.

In the early 1980s the Office of Fair Trading had decided to investigate the practices of the London Stock Exchange. The Trade & Industry Secretary Cecil Parkinson and Chancellor Nigel Lawson argued that the City should be allowed to reform itself. The failure to have a public body carry out its inquiry, gather evidence and hear from witnesses, and then publish a public report meant the practices of the City would stay shrouded in mystery for most of the media and the population.

The self-regulation was enshrined in law through the Financial Services Act 1986. This allowed the institutions of the City to set their own rules and oversee them. A number of self-regulatory organisations (SROs), for each area of financial service, were established. As the Chancellor who guided the Act through Parliament later noted, "the SROs did not always prove as vigilant against fraudsters as might have been hoped"[49] – hardly unexpected if you allow the children to be in charge of the sweet jar. However, the flaws in this inherently weak regulatory framework were attributed instead to some temporary exuberance: "it was inevitable that a time of boom and optimism such as the second half of the 1980s should see such an upsurge in financial fraud".[50] It is hard to imagine a senior government minister ever being so blasé about benefit fraud, but one is a crime committed by the poor, the other by the rich.

One of the first moves of the New Labour government was to implement the policy long advocated by Nigel Lawson to make the Bank of England independent. This was about placing key parts of monetary policy at least one remove from democratic oversight. Revealing the anti-democratic logic of the move, Lawson argued, "politicians, however austere they may be, are subject to electoral pressures which will be thought, rightly or wrongly, to affect their judgement".[51] The message is clear: politicians should do what is in the interests of high finance, rather than act in response to the "electoral pressures" of the people who elect them to work in their interests.

It was in this same mindset that the Labour government set about further deregulation across business, including "the administration of tax". Setting up the system of financial sector regulation that would be in place at the time of the crash, then chancellor Gordon Brown said it would be "not just a light touch, but a limited touch".[52] In Brown's Treasury too, HM Revenue and Customs (HMRC) was being transformed. Case directors, who investigated transnational corporations became customer relationship managers. An HMRC informant told an investigator, "we used to have a priority to collect tax, now we have a priority to have a good relationship".[53] The House of Commons Public Accounts Committee found in 2007 that nearly one-third of the UK's 700 largest businesses paid no corporation tax in the 2005-06 tax year, and a similar number paid far less than was expected.

This relaxed attitude to corporations paying their tax interacted with the privatisation agenda in 2001, to create something that reads like a satire. Six hundred HMRC office buildings were sold off to a company called Mapeley, which then rented them back to the Treasury. Mapeley was registered in the tax haven of Bermuda to avoid tax. It was perhaps a metaphor for how deeply entrenched privatisation and deregulation were in the heart of government.

In 1984 the Conservative government halved the stamp duty on purchasing shares, and halved it again in 1986. This was partially to signify the clear aim of the Thatcher government to widen share ownership among the British population – something she marketed as 'popular capitalism' – but the main beneficiaries were the institutional investors who regularly bought and sold shares and in massive proportions. This was a tax cut for speculators in the finance sector. In 1979 individuals owned 28% of UK shares (by value), but by 2010, this had fallen to just 11.5% of UK shares. The reality of 'popular capitalism' became more mythical in the Thatcher years. It would more honestly have been described as 'unpopular capitalism' as the public then and now opposed the selling off of public assets through privatisation.

Due to the growth and deregulation of the finance sector, and the cut in tax rates, the rate of return on capital investment nearly doubled between 1984 and 1989. It was during this period that the venture capital industry (also known as private equity) emerged. By 1985 the UK venture capital sector was twice as large as in the rest of the EC (predecessor of the EU) combined. Private equity firms gained notoriety in the 2000s as large firms were bought out, brought into private ownership (way from public regulation) loaded with debts, and asset stripped for a quick profit. This was finance capital devouring productive capital, capitalism as cannibalism.

But it wasn't just private equity firms, though they were the most extreme examples, UK business culture became increasing focused on immediate returns. Creativity and innovation (the very things that free market advocates praise) often require patient, long-term investment in research and developing new products. According to Professor Richard Jones of Sheffield University, "in 1979 the UK was one of the most research-intensive economies in the world. Now, amongst the advanced industrial economies, it is one of the least".[54] Finance capital has sought out the fastest highest returns in often complex but socially useless markets. This has drawn investment away from long-term medium-return investment in developing and producing socially useful and economically stable goods and services. Without that investment, research budgets are cut and any good inventions that do emerge are likely to be developed in other countries rather than in the UK. With successive governments eschewing any industrial strategy – the money dried up for socially productive uses, and flooded into the destabilising, speculative activity of the money markets.

Conclusion

The faith in free market economics was evangelical and dogmatic. Nigel Lawson the chancellor who was architect of much of this shift confidently asserted in 1992 (when unemployment was over 2.75 million) that "the reforms of the 1980s have indeed improved the economy's long-term growth potential". However, this assertion is not borne out by the official data – which shows that between 1955 and the election of the Thatcher government, UK growth averaged 3.0% a year. From 1979 until 2013, it has averaged just 2.1%.[55]

Although it is significant that the Thatcher reforms – said to have unleashed dynamism and entrepreneurialism – led to lower growth, the significance of this period is not the emptiness of its own propaganda. What this period represented – later consolidated, reinforced and extended by successor governments – was a strengthening of the short-term profiteering part of the economy (represented by a deregulated finance sector) and the weakening of the government, the only economic force that can act in the long term public interest. The state was weakened in successive acts of self-harm by privatising its assets and reducing its tax revenues. By toughening the laws governing trade unions, the government also saw to it that workers' incomes declined as a proportion of national income, as a restraining force on the power of employers was weakened.

The dynamism unleashed by the 'great experiment' was not a liberated popular capitalism, but a deeply unequal and sclerotic economy that would lurch from crisis to ever larger crisis. It is no coincidence that the reforms made by the governments of Thatcher and Major – and maintained and even extended by those of Blair and Brown – brought the UK closer to the circumstances that prevailed in advance of the 1929 Wall Street crash which precipitated global economic havoc.

If you are wondering how the UK economy not only survived these reforms, and apparently thrived for some years after them, in the following chapter I will explain how these self-inflicted structural weaknesses were patched up and obscured from public view through a range of means.

3

The Illusion of an economy

In the last thirty-five years, politicians of all parties in government ceded power over fundamental sectors of our economy to a new oligarchy of corporations. This effectively ended what was a staple of every previous post-war government: an industrial strategy. In place of any strategy, politicians placed their faith in the alchemy of an ever more deregulated, liberalised, globalised and increasingly lightly taxed finance sector to deliver for the good of all.

Whereas governments had supported the development and maintenance of industry across the nation, from the 1980s the policy focus became whatever was necessary to attract even more of the finance sector to London, and then to do whatever it takes to keep it there. Shortly before becoming prime minister, then chancellor Gordon Brown addressed the City of London, boasting:

> "Now today over 40 per cent of the world's foreign equities are traded here, more than New York; over 30 per cent of the world's currencies exchanges take place here, more than New York and Tokyo combined; while New York and Tokyo are reliant mainly on their large American and Asian domestic markets, 80 per cent of our business is international; and in a study last week of the top 50 financial cities, the City of London came first".

A year earlier, Brown had been able to boast that the financial and business services sector was a larger share of our economy than in any other major economy. In contrast, manufacturing was devastated under the governments of Thatcher, Major, Blair and Brown alike. Since the early 1980s UK manufacturing has declined at twice the pace of even the US,[1] widely perceived to be the paragon of 'free market' economics. In contrast manufacturing accounted for a smaller share of the UK economy than in any other major competitor economy.

Two million manufacturing jobs were lost in the Thatcher years alone. This loss of jobs, skill and industry weakened our economy and devastated whole communities, but was dismissed by those in power as "a long overdue and badly needed onslaught on decades of overmanning".[2] The thesis that UK industry was overstaffed inherently believes that it is inefficient to have more people employed on a task than is absolutely necessary. This is what is meant when economic commentators refer to an industry as having low labour productivity – i.e. too little output per worker. To the profit-maximising capitalist this is an unacceptable state of affairs, as the same result can be achieved with fewer workers, and therefore at less expense to the capitalist (i.e. lower labour costs to eat into the owners' profit margins). So, in circumstances of overstaffing, the rational capitalist will sack excess workers and therefore enjoy a higher net rate of return from their investment (same returns, lower costs). This is perfectly logical. But the consequences should be of concern for the government (elected to act in the public interest) as in this instance the capitalist is simply externalising the costs to the state (and to us all collectively) through lost tax revenues from the workers laid off, and through the social security now payable to the unemployed workers. This is largely what happened in the 1980s: as trade union protections were eroded, state support for industries withdrawn, and a culture of 'greed is good' fostered, the state picked up an increasing bill for the failure of the economy to provide work for all those who needed it.

A high exchange rate – which provided a beneficial environment for the UK finance sector – was conversely helping to undermine the UK's manufacturing industry and costing jobs. The Confederation of British Industry (CBI) represents UK businesses. In 1980, before it reflected the growing dominance of the finance industry, it too was lobbying the Thatcher government to reduce the exchange rate of the pound, which had appreciated in value (relative to other currencies) by as much as 50%. On 30 March 1981, 364 economists wrote a letter to *The Times*, asserting that: "present policies will deepen the depression, erode the industrial base of our economy and threaten its social and political stability". A few months later riots swept several cities, while unemployment continued to rise until the latter half of 1986.

While there was a clear agenda to target some UK industries, such as coal-mining[3] – in order to break the industrial power of the workforce and its union – all industries were hit by the government's abdication of any responsibility for industry. The rationale was set out most eloquently by Nigel Lawson when defending the UK's trade deficit:

> "The obsession with the current balance of payments was a hangover from the period when the government was expected to manage the whole economy. A corollary of the switch to market ways of thinking in the 1980s should have been that the government was responsible for its own finances and the private sector for its finances".[4]

In short, the Thatcher government hoped the economy would become a private affair, not its responsibility. Government set increasingly low tax rates, increasingly diluted or removed regulations, and handed over management and responsibility for the economy to private businesses – with the explicit belief that what is good for business is good for the people and that all business needs to succeed is for government to get out of the way.

The abdication policy continued under New Labour, as one of Gordon Brown's first measures as Chancellor was to make the Bank of England independent. Not only was industry a private affair, even monetary policy was no longer a matter for government. This was a move advocated by Lawson, who explained that "unlike ministers, who are subject to political and electoral pressures, central bankers would be largely immune to such pressures".[5] The statement reflects a disregard, at worst contempt, for democracy. Why should the views of the public be taken into consideration? After all, the great leaders know best. If the current crisis has taught us anything, it should be that the powerful – be they politicians or bankers – have no monopoly on wisdom or competence. Across southern Europe, the latitude for central banks to dictate policy, immune from democratic and electoral pressures, has resulted in riots, economic collapse and even the suspension of electoral democracy.

Independence for the Bank of England – and for central banks generally – is key to establishing the ideological framework of free market capitalism as unchallengeable, by removing the question from democratic debate.

Rather than focusing on individual privatisations – like the railways or water industry – it is fair to say that our whole economic strategy has been largely privatised, franchised to the big banks and financial institutions. Interest rates, exchange rates and corporation tax rates have all been tailored to the needs of the finance sector. Government has become the servant, not the master, of corporate interests.

The social material needs of people – for jobs, decent incomes and homes, and for an economy that benefits them – are now the sole domain of social policy, and a cost to be borne and resented by government. Those unable to find employment are a burden. As Thatcher's chancellor declared "the promotion of jobs and employment is not the Treasury's principal responsibility ... the key to improved economic performance was allowing markets of all kinds to work better".[6] In the world outside the Treasury walls, it's hard to believe many of the rising number of unemployed people were saying, "I've lost my job, but I'm reassured the derivatives markets are working more efficiently", but then the economy was no longer being even remotely run in their interests.

The tensions in the UK economy between industry and finance are not new – indeed they date back to the early days of empire when Britain's imperial expansion led to investment in developing trading routes, infrastructure and industry abroad. So even at a time when Britain's industrial position was globally dominant, investment was not sufficiently directed into the domestic economy.

However, while these tensions have deep roots, the reforms of the Thatcher government – maintained and even modestly extended by successor governments – decisively resolved those tensions in favour of the finance sector. This sowed the seeds for the crisis to come, with asset price inflations bubbles driving growth interspersed by regular and intensifying debt crises as the bubble burst.

Despite overseeing the legislative changes that embraced this process, Nigel Lawson accurately assesses the result, albeit with a high level of cognitive dissonance:

> "Since the international debt problem of the early 1980s and the more general problems of banking and corporate indebtedness, which emerged a decade later, the possibility of a systemic collapse has been lurking in the background".[7]

However, while systemic collapse lurked and was acknowledged in private, successive governments continued to exacerbate its likelihood, and reduce its ability to resolve any crises, by continuing to surrender what levers they possessed to exercise any control over the economy.

While the UK government's role in the economy was being dismantled, governments of the eighties, nineties and noughties found ways to paper over the cracks and give the illusion of having a stable, dynamic and growing economy.

Everything must go! The great UK sale

Harold MacMillan's description of the privatising UK industry and infrastructure as, "Selling the family silver" (page 26) is very apt. Many of us have some level of household wealth – whether its jewellery, a car, a stamp collection, antiques or simply the home itself. These have value, they are assets.

The Thatcher and Major governments especially – and to a lesser extent the governments of Blair and Brown – sold off the UK family's silver. They were asset-strippers. They got into power and allowed the best bits of our nation to be looted. It was the economic burglary of the UK: our electricity, gas, water, telecommunications, the railways, postal service have all been sold off on the cheap.

The right-to-buy policy – in which council house tenants could buy their properties at knock-down prices – was perhaps the electoral jewel in the crown of Thatcher's government. Council tenants had assured tenancies meaning they could not be ousted from their homes except by a court order or by voluntarily surrendering their tenancy, but the right-to-buy policy essentially incentivised people to be fellow participants in the asset stripping of the UK.

The government restricted councils' borrowing powers and

ensured that the council housing stock sold could not replaced. The number of families on council housing waiting lists meanwhile rose, languishing at an astonishing 1.8 million in 2012.

The architects of the mass privatisation of the 1980s were under no delusion, "proceeds from privatisation – and for that matter council house sales – were bound to dry up once all saleable assets had eventually been realised".[8] Those who started the policy knew they would leave office having used one-off revenues, leaving subsequent governments to fill the revenue gap. It's rather like tenants renting a furnished property, and then paying the rent by selling the furnishings. That of course would be illegal, but the asset-stripping of the UK is no less criminal.

In the year following Thatcher's enforced departure, the UK economy was running a growing deficit, with privatisation proceeds only able to plug one-third of the spending gap. The economy was a mess, and even the panic sale of our most valuable assets could not fill the gap.

A similar scenario was to play out in the final months of the New Labour government under Gordon Brown's premiership. Just as Thatcher bagged up the family silver and flogged it at knock-down prices, so Brown and his Chancellor Alastair Darling scraped around for any valuable bits that Thatcher and Major had overlooked. And so on 12 October 2009, following several bank bailouts, Gordon Brown announced the great New Labour asset sale, "everything must go!" The announcement included the Royal Mint, Royal Mail, the Ordnance Survey, the Channel Tunnel Rail Link, and the Student Loan Book.

The flaw, as with his predecessors' privatisations, is that these government controlled assets are exactly that: assets. They generate income into the Exchequer, so Brown's action, although on a lesser scale, still met John McDonnell's devastating criticism of the Thatcher years (page 28) "slaughtering geese that lay golden eggs, for a one-day fry-up".

The table below shows the level of revenue that some of these assets – listed by Brown for privatisation – generated to the Exchequer every year, as the table below shows:

Organisation	Turnover	Surplus
Ordnance Survey	£117m	£16m (13.7%)
Royal Mint	£159m	£5m (2.9%)
Tote	£2,900m	£156m (5.4%)
Royal Mail	£9,560m	£321m (3.4%)
Dartford Crossing	£23m	£4m (17.7%)
Urenco (1/3rd)	£1,130m	£240m (21.2%)

In addition the Student Loan Company received £900 million in 2008/09 in student loan repayments. Even without taking into consideration the revenue generated by some of the proposed asset sales (e.g. the Channel Tunnel Rail Link), we can see that these raise around £1.5 billion per year for the Exchequer. It would therefore make no sense to sell these assets. Instead the opposite is true – they demonstrate the case for creating more revenue generating assets in public ownership.

Gordon Brown had little chance to implement his privatisation programme as Labour lost the 2010 election, but a contrasting decision taken by Brown's government the year before shows the benefit of changing direction. In 2009, the east coast mainline rail franchise collapsed, and was brought into public ownership. Between 2009 and 2013 it generated £800 million for the UK exchequer. Despite this great return, the coalition government announced its intention to re-privatise the franchise.

As noted previously, council housing is a large income generator. This is why the private sector is keen to get its hands on it – and Brown was only too happy to oblige. His £16 billion asset sale announcement in October 2009 included the sale of a further tens of thousands of council homes. As another Labour backbencher, Jeremy Corbyn MP, commented at the time, "to sell assets means a loss of already huge public investments and enables the purchaser to fleece the public for decades to come" – which is of course why they are 'assets' and why private profiteers are keen to grab them. Although council homes sold under right-to-buy are bought by their tenants, one-third of those sold in the 1980s are now owned by private landlords.

Brown's proposed asset sales, like those of his predecessors, made no economic sense. They would have damaged government revenues in the medium and long term, while providing only a short-term fillip.

Since the election of the Conservative government in 2010, the privatisation frenzy has continued. Royal Mail was privatised on the cheap, in the face of opposition from Royal Mail staff, the public and – in a u-turn on previous policy – the Labour Party. The sell-off highlighted, like those in the 1980s, how the government had failed to value the company accurately. The government took an asset built up over generations by mail users and workers, and us all as taxpayers, and sold it off on the cheap. Those who profited the most were those who could afford to buy the most shares. The rich made a fortune, the government lost a revenue stream, and we all lost a public asset.

Guzzling at the pipe: getting high on North Sea Oil

Despite the recession into which the Thatcher government plunged the UK in the early 1980s and the relatively anaemic growth that followed, something remarkable was achieved in those first six years – the national debt fell.

The 'get out of jail free card' for Mrs Thatcher's government was North Sea oil. Following several discoveries in the late 1960s and early 1970s, the North Sea's 'black gold' became a major part of the UK economy and its energy provision. Governments were keen to exploit the lucrative oil (and gas) finds. As Thatcher's Chancellor reflected, "it is to a large extent a windfall, yielding a surplus well above production costs – a fact reflected in the special tax regime imposed to capture a large part of that windfall".[9] And it was the Thatcher government that inherited the windfall. Revenues from UK gas and oil production leapt by over 300% from £565 million in 1978/79 to £2.3 billion in 1979/80. By the mid-1980s oil and gas production netted £12 billion a year to the Treasury, to paper over the cracks of Thatcher and Lawson's failing experiment.[10]

Although revenues have declined from that peak, even thirty years after the initial discoveries, in 1999, the UK was producing more oil than Iraq, Kuwait or Nigeria. However, at some point around then, Britain went from being comfortably self-sufficient in oil and gas to being a net importer. Like a spoilt brat spending their parents' wealth, the UK's oil and gas inheritance was running out. Despite all the talk of 'economic dynamism' under Thatcher, and 'prudence' under Gordon Brown, the reality is that the UK's dirty little secret was that oil was being poured over the troubled waters of the UK's economy. The economics correspondent of *The Guardian*, Larry Elliott, says the history of the UK and North Sea oil can be summed up in just three words: "discovered, extracted, squandered."[11]

Adjusted for inflation, in a little under forty years the North Sea oil and gas production alone has generated revenues for government in excess of £180 billion – which in itself would account for over one-eighth of all economic growth in that period – and that ignores the revenue raised through additional employment and supply chain businesses.

For an idea of how different things could have been it is instructive to look at the contrasting path taken by our North Sea neighbour Norway. Whereas successive UK chancellors saw oil revenues as an opportunity to fund temporary largesse (normally, tax cuts for the rich), in Norway a proportion of these time-limited revenues was put aside into a fund to invest in new technologies and industries. As the Sky News economics editor Ed Conway wrote in the *Telegraph* in 2009, "treating the oil money as a permanent asset rather than a temporary benefit has left us ill-prepared for its decline".[12] Although North Sea oil revenues continue to generate considerable government income, that will fall from £6.5 billion in 2012-2013 to £3.9 billion by 2017-18.[13] The UK now faces a future where it no longer holds reserves of gas and oil, has closed its coal mines, has ageing nuclear power infrastructure, and lags far behind most other countries in terms of investment in sustainable renewable technologies. A UK energy crisis is a rapidly approaching reality.

By contrast, Norway has the world's largest sovereign wealth fund (known until 2006 as the 'Petroleum Fund of Norway'), estimated in May 2013 as being worth £478 billion – about one and a half times the country's GDP, equating to nearly £100,000 for every man, woman and child in Norway. The fund receives revenues from Norwegian oil and gas extraction, and from the dividends of the majority government owned oil company, Statoil – as, unlike the UK government, the Norwegians did not sell off their assets for short term gain.

The UK therefore faces the coming period with no more major revenues from mineral wealth, a relatively weak manufacturing sector, and massive consumer, corporate and government debts. This is the traumatic consequence of a political culture that eschews any economic growth strategy, other than the potentially disastrous hope of another credit or asset price boom, while denying the resultant trauma that inevitably brings.

The nineties into the noughties: Debt and the Credit boom

The story of the 1990s recovery was in fact a reality of debt-fuelled consumption. People were not 'living within their means'. The figures are shocking: by 2006 the average British adult had debts worth 163% of their income. This was mostly not due to the familiar yarn told by politicians and media commentators – that flat screen TVs, two foreign holidays a year, and a new car every three years had become the new normal.

In fact, it was very much the basic costs of living that had driven much of the increase. The massive rise in housing costs (both rents and new mortgages) meant more of people's earnings were spent just keeping a roof over their heads.

But the housing bubble tells only half the story, the other half concerns our wages. Even in the 'boom years' before the great experiment failed, the value of people's pay packets was declining in real terms.

To explain this very simply, inflation (the collated change in cost of what we buy) was rising more quickly than people's wages or benefits. The cost of the same things you spent your income on last year went up at a higher rate than your wages the following year. To meet that shortfall people borrowed. At the lower end of the income scale people went to loan sharks and payday loan companies, on middle incomes people took out secured loans or re-mortgaged cheaply against their rising home values. It all added up to more debt. Once you have debts, they need to be serviced, so more of your income is taken up paying debt interest. In other words more of your income is going to the banks, rather than more productive parts of the economy.

On the eve of the crisis, the UK public was more indebted than any other in Europe or North America. But it wasn't just consumer debt.

British companies had also amassed a shocking stockpile of corporate debt that even exceeded that taken on by UK households. The UK corporate sector used their easier access to credit on financial takeovers and overseas investment rather than in improving domestic infrastructure and creating jobs. Investing for higher and quicker returns was part of the late 1980s culture of short-term profit over long-term strategy. And at the same time private equity companies asset-stripped other companies and loaded them with debts.

In 2010 total UK debt – personal, corporate and government – stood at 540% of the total value of what the UK produced in a year. Just over twenty years previously its total debt was just 200%. The change is most stark in the financial sector, which accountants PWC estimated to have risen "from 46% of GDP in 1987 to 245% in 2009".[14]

Debt had become big business. The deregulation of the finance sector meant money poured into this largely unregulated field. The payday loan companies, characterised by campaigners as legal loan sharks, commonly charged interest rates of over 1000% per annum, and in some cases over 4000%. The banks generally gave interest rates on savings far lower than even the lowest interest rate offered to the most secure borrowers.

The drying up of council housing, meant more and more people were forced into debt to meet their rental costs, and more and more people scrabbled together what they could to get a mortgage. Banks obliged and offered larger and larger mortgages to people who two decades ago would have been refused.

Far from education being "a gift from one generation to another", as the Labour MP John McDonnell described it, the New Labour government of Tony Blair decided to gradually redefine university education as an investment. Students were to be loaded with debts in the hope their investment (formerly known as education) would pay off in the long run. No one told them the small print, 'earnings may go up or down' as a result of a university education.

A new generation left university from 2001 onwards and saw their incomes hit with an extra 9% tax to repay their debts. Their disposable incomes, and ability to save for a mortgage, constrained by their debts.

The economist Graham Turner sums up the debt boom, "credit was needed to fill the gap left by stagnant wages and a three-decades-long assault on organised labour".[15] But an economy based on debt-financed spending is inherently unstable. Consumers cannot go on borrowing more indeterminably. The debt either has to be repaid, which suppresses consumer spending as the debt is repaid (this is technically known as 'deleveraging') or consumers default on their borrowing – which means their debts are so great that they can no longer meet the repayments. When consumers default on loans and mortgages (i.e. declare themselves bankrupt or insolvent) on a mass scale then the lending institutions are likely to go bust as well – as happened most spectacularly in the US housing market in 2006-08.

Many economists now describe the long boom period from the mid-1990s until 2007 as a debt-financed bubble. The longer the boom, the more the debt bubble inflates, the bigger the problem when it bursts, and the longer it will take to recover. When a debt-financed bubble bursts the recovery is slow as businesses and individuals deleverage (i.e. slowly pay back their debts and build up their savings) and banks sift through the balance sheets after the multiple defaults. With hindsight, the banks see the error of this irresponsible lending and tighten lending criteria to consumers and businesses. The banks also increase interest rates, partially to more accurately reflect the risks of lending but mostly to increase their rate of profit to compensate for lower volumes of lending and to strengthen their reserves.

Missing the early warning

The recession of the early 1990s – the bursting of a debt-financed housing bubble – was a precursor of the larger collapse that was to follow 15 years later. The architect of this financial deregulation reports that lenders suffered "unprecedented bad debts" – those were pennies down the back of the sofa compared to the gargantuan losses faced in 2008.

In the years preceding the recession (the 'Lawson boom'), economic growth averaged over 4% a year. There was some temporary relief for manufacturing too as following years of the UK pound strengthening against foreign currencies (due to the rapid growth of the finance sector), the pound weakened dramatically in 1986. The UK share of global manufacturing output had plummeted from 4.5% in 1980 to 3.4% in 1985, but by the last full year of the boom, it had recovered to 4.3%.[16]

The devaluation of the pound (a correction to its over-inflated value) was also a key part of the Lawson boom. But it was the deregulation of credit and tax breaks for property purchases that assisted the most spectacular housing bubble in UK history – by the end of 1988, house prices had risen by an average of 30%.

With hindsight Lawson was sanguine, conceding that what was often termed the 'Lawson boom' "led too many borrowers and lenders to believe that it would go on forever, and that the economic cycle, with its alternation of upswing and downswing, was a thing of the past. This was the fatal error".[17]

That 'fatal error' should have been learned from by his longest-serving successor, Gordon Brown, who instead repeated his delusion, proclaiming in his final 2007 Budget speech "we will never return to the old boom and bust". Both Lawson and Brown fell prey to the delusion JK Galbraith identified in his 1955 book on the 1929 Wall Street Crash.

The 1990s recession could have been the lesson to prevent the slump that followed the 2008 crash – it was almost a preview of the bigger shock to follow. Mortgage lenders then had upped their lending multiples – instead of lending at two-and-a-half or three times people's earnings, they started lending at (then unprecedented) multiples of three-and-a-half or four times income. Likewise the 100% mortgage (i.e. with no deposit) also emerged for the first time.

The housing bubble, which saw house prices increase by 70% in the final four years of the 1980s, was the result of a combination of policies. The housing market was expanded by the right-to-buy scheme, tax breaks were given for those developing property portfolios, and lending restrictions were either loosened or abolished altogether. Despite the crash of the early 1990s, the causes of which were readily understood, nothing was done to change the regulatory framework. The inherent risks within such a deregulated economy just had to be accepted as the norm, as Nigel Lawson reflected in 1992: "a financially deregulated economy, while more efficient and dynamic, is also probably less stable".[18] What Lawson doesn't factor into his calculations is that instability (and its consequences) somewhat undermines claims for efficiency or any sort of dynamism that would be welcome.

This instability was evident from the credit bubble that underpinned the housing bubble. Lending increased at a rate of about 20% per year throughout the 1980s, plunging when the crash took hold in the early 1990s. The credit and housing bubbles reinforced each other. As house prices inflated, so homeowners borrowed more and spending increased. Homeowners borrowed through easier credit secured against their home, and more credit due to the rising value of their home.

As Nigel Lawson said, his 'credit revolution' "allowed people, to an unprecedented and unknown extent, to bring their spending forward, ahead of their incomes".[19] This was bound to end in disaster.

Finance is king

Having hollowed out our industrial base, the great experiment had left but one growth industry in the UK: finance.

Our politicians became 'evangelists' for the finance sector – so much so that they failed to believe there was any difference between the returns it brought and those from manufacturing, retail, agriculture or any other sector.

The finance sector had been transformed though. It was no longer a means of supporting the economy, it was the economy. Our services sector was dependent on the supply of cheap credit to keep us spending (replacing the need for real wage increases), the housing market was now an investment game, and speculation on debts became a business in itself. An army of accountants and advisers assisted the rich in avoiding paying their taxes (meaning tax-funded public services saw little of the gains from the finance boom).

The public assets that had been privatised were now companies whose shares were traded in the finance sector. Long-term investment became a thing of the past, as the need to make ever more profit became paramount. Instead of being run in the public interest, the water and energy companies operated to maximise profits for a few. UK investment in renewable energy lagged behind every other major economy, while our bills rose higher and higher. Hosepipe bans became a regular occurrence, as reservoirs and surrounding land was sold off to make a quick buck – and of course bills rose way above inflation.

Privatisation meant the loss of income streams for government. The one-off gains from asset sales have to be considered against a lifetime loss of revenue. Assets that were built and invested in over generations were cast off for a pre-election giveaway here, a corporate tax cut there.

Investment bankers were feted in political and media circles as if they held some mystical oracle quality – and not just on matters of finance, the Labour government asked an investment banker, David Freud, to write their welfare policy. Freud went on to become a Lord, a Conservative minister and was the architect of the 'bedroom tax' – one of the most deeply unpopular policies of the coalition government.

The spectacle of an investment banker making decisions about the living standards of the poorest is the apogee of a society in which the rich are lauded for being rich and poor demeaned for being poor.

Individual greed was lauded and applauded. The rich became known as 'wealth creators'- and they were, if only for themselves. In their wake though workers laid off, those struggling to pay their bills or their rent, young people unable to buy their first home, and the elderly dying in winter because they couldn't afford to heat their homes. A wealth of struggle and misery for the many to facilitate a wealth of riches for the few.

But it wasn't just a collective sense of society that was breaking down. What we were witnessing was the cannibalism of the UK economy, which was systematically eating itself. It was brutal, unsustainable and would inevitably leave a bloody mess.

The City of London was at the heart of this cannibal capitalism. The deregulation of finance capital, following Lawson's 'Big Bang' left the City like an "internal offshore island" according to anti-tax haven campaigner and author Nicholas Shaxson, who explains the UK economy "sits spider-like, at the centre of a vast international web of tax havens, hoovering up trillions of dollars of business and capital from around the globe".[20]

Finance isn't just another industry, like shipbuilding or biotechnology. In the finance sector success was measured by how far regulation and taxation could be avoided or undermined. Making the finance sector king meant it controlled economic policy. What was in the interests of the bankers, became the 'national interest'.

One of the few people in Parliament to be a critical voice of Labour's continuation of Thatcher's economic revolution was Labour backbencher John McDonnell MP. He was interviewed about the bank bailout on Sky News on 8 October 2008. His immediate analysis of unfolding events was, in hindsight, remarkable:

"I think this is a really poor deal. We're putting up £50 billion of taxpayers' money, we're getting preference shares with no votes so therefore no controlling interest. We can't even put people on their boards. The preference shares will be bought in those banks who really need it and are the ones with the dodgiest debts. So we're nationalising the loss-making banks, by the looks of it in partial form. But in addition to that what it will mean is that for this deal we'll have to increase our borrowing, which means putting up taxes, which also means cuts in public expenditure, reducing demand in the economy – and which will deepen and lengthen the recession. So my constituents will pay for this deal with their taxes and as a result of the recession with the loss of jobs and some of them with the loss of their homes. So I think this is a very poor deal."

"This is like your next door neighbour having a binge party, buying a new car, going on holiday and then sending you the bill and expecting you to pick up the tab. That's what the government is expecting the taxpayer to do without any control about what will happen in the future. I don't think that's an acceptable deal."[21]

This was the result of making finance king. As we saw in chapter 1, when the crash happened, Parliament scrambled around to find a solution that would save the king. Public money – previously unavailable for students or pensioners – was found, and by the bucket-load, for the banks. I asked John McDonnell what it was like as ministers and opposition MPs came to terms with the crumbling of their financial system. He replied, "They were panicking, and clueless because they had put so much faith in the City. They were frightened of the City and in awe."

Postscript – a system exposed

After the global financial system had crashed economies around the world, it would seem obvious that the system would face substantial reform (at the very least) to ensure that nothing like this could happen again.

And like a major earthquake, the credit crunch was surrounded by several tremors before and after – exposing further corruption and fraud that had become institutionalised within the system.

One such fraud was payment protection insurance (PPI), which bank customers were sold when they took out loans, mortgages or credit cards. The idea of PPI was that it would ensure that your debts were paid should you lose your job and your income fall. But in 2008 consumer rights magazine *Which?* estimated that as many as one-third of the policies sold may have been sold to people who would be ineligible to make a claim (as they were pensioners, self-employed or on a fixed term contract). Many more were also sold without the consumer being told that the insurance was optional.

The now defunct Financial Services Authority (FSA) started imposing fines for mis-selling in 2006, but the tide of complaints by victims has now become a tsunami. In the first half of 2013 alone, over 280,000 new complaints of PPI mis-selling were reported to the financial ombudsman. In total over £18 billion has been set aside by the banks in PPI compensation.

It is now the biggest mis-selling scandal in UK financial history. It is important to note that banks were not just playing the system in the regulatory netherworld of the global derivatives markets, but at home on the high street too, the banks were scamming their own customers – with the FSA estimating that 3 million of people in the UK could have been mis-sold.

So the banks were defrauding their customers as well as other banks by mis-selling rubbish products too complex for the buyer to understand – whether that was PPIs or CDOs. But the banks were also defrauding the government, by assisting the super-rich and big business to avoid paying their taxes. In doing so, they were ripping off every UK taxpayer – by leaving them to shoulder a larger tax burden as they helped the rich and powerful to shirk their responsibilities. This causes taxes to rise on the rest of us in relatively rich nations like the UK. In developing countries it means people die. The international aid charity ActionAid says, "Every year developing countries lose billions of pounds of vitally needed revenue because of tax avoidance by big companies using tax havens... they drain billions of pounds of revenues out of developing countries that could be used to help build schools and hospitals and lift people out of poverty".[22]

At Barclays bank an entire unit was established to assist in tax dodging. The structured capital markets division was finally shut down in early 2013. Its prime purpose was to help its clients to avoid tax. It generated a £1 billion annual profit for Barclays in so doing, although it is impossible to calculate how many billions have been denied to government revenues around the world to fund healthcare, education, or to pay pensions and social security. Barclays itself engaged in some creative accounting of its own – in 2012 paying just £82m in UK tax on profits of £7 billion, an effective tax rate of just over 1%.

One product marketed by Barclays was known as Stars – which stood for structured trust advantaged repackaged securities. We only know about this because of a US court case which found Stars to be "an abusive tax avoidance scheme" and concluding the action of those "who were involved in this and other transactions was nothing short of reprehensible". At stake was $660 million of

US tax revenues. In a similar episode in 2012, with £500 million of UK revenues at stake, Barclays was slapped down by Treasury minister David Gauke MP, who lamented:

> "The bank that disclosed these schemes to HM Revenue & Customs has adopted the Banking Code of Practice on Taxation which contains a commitment not to engage in tax avoidance. The government is clear that these are not transactions that a bank that has adopted the code should be undertaking."

So in the UK banks merely have a code to sign up to committing them to not ripping off the public purse. This code was introduced in 2009, and it allows banks to disclose schemes without any risk of fine, penalty or prosecution. There are no plans to introduce similar disclosure codes for shoplifters, benefit cheats, or fare dodgers – they will continue to be prosecuted for ripping off public and private purses. These complex tax avoidance schemes are ongoing, highly profitable to the banks and leave the Treasury playing catch up.

Of course the banks also engage in outright criminality too – for which HSBC has recently been fined. The banks were found to be laundering money for gangsters and criminals like Mexican drug barons, as well as flouting international sanctions to launder Iran's oil revenues. A 330 page report by the US Senate Committee on Homeland Security and Governmental Affairs accused HSBC of "a failure to monitor $60 trillion in wire transfer and account activity... [and] a backlog of 17,000 unreviewed account alerts regarding potentially suspicious activity".[23] As a result, HSBC was fined almost $2 billion by US authorities.

The picture is becoming clear, left to their own devices the banks institutionally default to a philosophy of 'whatever we can get away with'. In the UK, a still emerging scandal is the manipulation of Libor – the London interbank offered rate. Libor is an interest rate used by banks for transactions between each other. It also influences the cost of borrowing charged to small businesses and consumers. Because of the way Libor is calculated – averaging out the interest rates of several banks (and excluding the highest and lowest outliers) and the manipulation of Libor must involve a cartel-like operation: a group of banks acting together to raise or lower the rate to increase their profits. Publishing a low rate also indicated that a bank was seen as a 'safe bet', in that it could borrow cheaply at low interest rates. As the banking crisis unfurled, it was important to some institutions to appear more secure than they actually were (so as not to cause panic) and there is evidence that some banks lowered their rate to give a false impression of stability. UK banks implicated in the scandal include RBS (which became 83% publicly owned), Barclays as well as UK broker ICAP – all of whom have already paid fines.

Today, the UK banks are attempting to recapitalise. Fines for misconduct and mis-selling, as well as toxic debts due to unwise lending and trading, have hit the banks' balance sheets. One way the UK banks have attempted to do this is by increasing the margin between the interest rate offered to savers and the interest rate charged to borrowers. In 2012 the UK banks offered an average 0.9% interest rate on bank deposits but charged an average 3.9% to borrowers. By contrast, banks in the Eurozone offered an interest rate of 2.0% on bank deposits, while lending at an average of 3.6%. The margin offered by the UK banks was almost twice as great. Perfectly legal, but perhaps indicative that for all the talk of global competition – the philosophy of the UK banks remains 'whatever we can get away with'.

The blame for this cannot lie solely at the door of the banks. In democracies we elect governments to operate in our interests. Our politicians have failed to act in our interests, and failed to stand up to the banks – most obviously pre-crisis, but perhaps more surprisingly they have failed to stand up to them post-crisis either.

This is not simply a financial failure, but a failure of our democracy, of our politics – admittedly manifested very visibly through the financial sector crash. While many people paid the price through unemployment, reduced incomes, higher borrowing rates, lower savings rates, and the resultant austerity chipping away at their public services, the failure of politicians to even begin to reform the system beyond a few gimmicks has meant the banks have had a rather good crisis.

According to the European Banking Authority there were 3,530 bankers receiving more than €1 million in 2012. The UK, just one of 31 Europeans countries covered by the EBA survey, accounted for 2,714 or 77% of those bankers.[24]

Germany, with a larger economy less impacted by the global financial crash, has only 212 bankers earning in excess of €1 million a year. This is less than 8% of the UK total – and Germany's millionaire bankers also earn less on average than their UK counterparts. It is clear that a large successful economy does not require this level of banking industry, but in the UK finance is king.

I hope by now you feel some affinity with the words of the great English economist John Maynard Keynes, who following the second world war negotiated the international finance arrangements that have now been dismantled:

> "The decadent international but individualistic capitalism
> ... is not a success. It is not intelligent, it is not beautiful,
> it is not just, it is not virtuous. And it does not deliver
> the goods. In short, we dislike it, and we are beginning to
> despise it."[25]

In the following chapter I analyse the state of our economy post-crisis, and argue that finance should be dethroned. Chapter 5 looks at the democratic regime that could take its place.

4

The state of our economy

Whereas chapter two looked at how the seeds of the economic crash were sown, this chapter looks at the poisonous legacy and deep structural problems that remain in the UK economy. In identifying the economic problems this chapter also identifies the political failures too, and is therefore a prelude to the final chapter on what democratic changes need to build an economy as if people mattered.

The failure of financialisation

As the financial sector grew to become ever more dominant in the UK economy, its immense economic and political power skewed the rest of the economy too. It sucked investment away from socially useful parts of the economy, and directed it into "socially useless activity", as Lord Adair Turner, former CBI director-general and chair of the banking regulator Financial Services Authority, described it. The sole 'benefit' of this activity has been to enrich a tiny elite. When this system collapsed it required a series of massive public bailouts, which the governor of the Bank of England, Mervyn King, characterised by saying, "Never in the field of financial endeavour, has so much money been owed by so few to so many". King went on, "And, one might add, so far with little real reform".[1] His words in 2009 remain as true today, and perfectly illustrate the gaping void in UK politics created by a political consensus between the major parties that fundamentally offer no alternative concept about how the UK economy could be run.

Major economies all over the world have banking sectors, but none grew as large and powerful as in the UK. Even post-crash, UK banks in 2011 held more assets than banks in any other EU country – over 16% more than Germany, the largest economic power in Europe, with an economy one and a half times as large as the UK. However, German banks employed 50% more staff than UK banks and had over four times as many branches. So in terms of the banking you and I do, German banks probably offer a far more convenient and accessible service than we in the UK receive.

The explanation for this is that UK banks' primary function is not to support the domestic market of individual consumers and small businesses, but to generate large returns through speculative trading in the international financial markets, generating large bonuses for those involved. Even locally, banks see higher returns not from investing in local businesses but from inflating house prices in the UK's dysfunctional housing market. On the UK high street, the rapacious attitude of UK banking is also seen in the replacement of bank staff with self-service machines, with longer queues for those who need assistance.

In each of the ten years between 2003 to 2012, German banks (with smaller assets) lent 42% more to non-financial companies than UK banks. So where did UK banks lending go? They lent five times as much as German banks for house purchase (mortgages), and in the five years leading up to the crash (2003-2007) lent 16% more in consumer credit.[2] When you consider that Germany has a population of around 18 million more people (about 30% larger) than the UK, then those figures are even more extreme.

That extremity is also a lingering source of fragility in the economy. Estimates in 2012 by the OBR reveal that the planned UK economic recovery is based upon increasing household expenditure, without a commensurate rise in incomes, so that personal debt will grow by nearly 50% to over £2 trillion by 2015. Even before that consumer debt is higher in the UK than in any comparable national economy – higher than in the US, China, Japan, Germany or France. With UK households so indebted and with falling real incomes, the slightest of economic downturns could cause a new round of debt defaults sending the banks and the economy into a new crisis.

The UK finance sector works, not as a support mechanism to the economy, but in its own interests alone to create huge profits for a few. But in doing so it creates equally huge damages – inflating house prices, driving down wages, cutting and offshoring jobs, and denying investment to socially useful and employment creating industries. The modus operandi of the UK banks make economic problems, and even crises, inevitable.

The financialisation of the UK economy has caused systematic damage. It channels capital away from investment that creates jobs, which improves productivity through investment in new technology and in the research and development that produces new technology. According to Professor Richard Jones of Sheffield University, "in 1979 the UK was one of the most research-intensive economies in the world. Now, amongst the advanced industrial economies, it is one of the least".[3] Finance capital has sought out the fastest highest returns in often complex but socially useless speculative markets. This has drawn capital away from the patient investment needed to identify innovative new products and inventions.

Hand in hand with the decline in research and development investment has gone the decline in UK industry. Manufacturing is a smaller share of the UK economy than in any of the other major economies of the world. From employing six million people in the late 1970s, manufacturing employs only around two million today (though some of that decline is inevitably due to new technology replacing the need for workers). But since the financial crash, the value of the UK pound in global trade has declined further than in previous recessions, and yet UK exports have not been significantly boosted because of the thirty years of shrinkage in UK manufacturing.

Today the UK has a huge trade deficit, which hit a 24-year high of £21 billion in December 2013, but the UK has been in deficit with the rest of the world every year since 1983.[4] When politicians talked post-crash about an export-led recovery, they were fantasising – especially since they offered no policies to actually rebuild UK manufacturing.

In its place, private consumption has grown from 55% of the UK economy in the 1970s, rising to 58% in the 1980s, peaking at over 65% pre-crash, before dropping back marginally to 62.5% in 2011.[5] Governments have made no attempt to redress this trend, merely shifted taxation towards consumption (VAT, the tax on what we consume, has risen from 8 to 12.5% in the late 1970s to 20% since 2010) reflecting the increasing hollowing out of UK manufacturing. In March 2012, the Office for Budget Responsibility forecasted that between 2010/11 to 2016/17 government revenues from income tax would rise 33.9%, from national insurance 36.1%, and VAT by 40.7%. In contrast revenues from corporation tax would rise only by 14.9%.[6] So the burden of taxation continues to shift from business to the individual.

In place of an industrial strategy successive governments have, to attract companies to invest in the UK, fetishised tax breaks and corporation tax cuts which reduce government revenues from these sources and push the tax burden further onto the shoulders of the general public.

UK infrastructure – our transport, energy and communications networks, as well as our public services – has also missed out on investment and so UK companies struggle to compete internationally with expensive domestic energy and transport costs. Likewise, despite the lax tax regime, transnational companies often choose to invest in other countries that have modern infrastructure. This makes the UK a far less attractive place for non-financial global businesses to invest. According to the World Bank the UK ranks seventh in the world as a place to do business, but our infrastructure is only ranked at 24th in the world.

The failure of our national infrastructure

Infrastructure is important, but when it works well we shouldn't really notice it. Good transport, communications and energy networks make our lives easier, save us time and save us money. Bad infrastructure does the opposite.

As government has increasingly privatised our infrastructure it has ceded the power to force infrastructure investment. And by failing to put clear regulations on those industries in the public interest, governments have allowed the new private owners to simply leech huge profits, while failing to invest and develop our national infrastructure for the future.

As a result, there is a declining level of investment in the economy and no industrial strategy in its place. This privatisation of industrial policy is evident from the chart (see over), which clearly dates the economic shift that took place with the election of the Thatcher government, and which has been maintained by its successors.

This is a giant void where government should be acting in the public interest, but the government is not only the architect of the void but still believes the void is the correct path. As the chart shows (over), government investment in the economy has continued to fall post-crash too. Despite being able to borrow cheaply following the crash, the coalition government cut its investment. It has though, in the coalition government's defence,

Government investment in the UK economy as a % of GDP

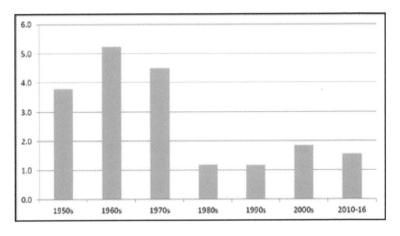

Source: HM Treasury, Public Finances Databank[7]

significantly scaled back its spending through PFI – though the legacy of that debt remains, weighing down on investment and causing cutbacks in areas like the NHS. But what can't be defended is that the government has failed to fill the gap left by PFI. So while public investment was 3.4% of GDP in 2009/10, in the five years from 2013/14 it is not budgeted to reach even half that level.[8]

It is often said that it is 'not the role of government to pick winners and losers', and that innovation is best left to the dynamism of the private sector. Nothing could be further from the truth. The patient investment in research and development necessary for developing major new innovations is not best provided for those looking for quick high returns. As Professor Mariana Mazzucato, author of *The Entrepreneurial State*,[9] points out:

> "All the most important technologies that have driven growth – what economists call general purpose technologies – trace their funding back to government

... and nurture decades of growth. These include aviation technologies, space technologies, semiconductors, the Internet, nuclear power, and nanotechnology".[10]

It may be that the private sector has been highly efficient at moulding these technologies into desirable products and marketing them to us, but it is governments (mostly not the UK government in recent times) that have funded the innovations.

Modern infrastructure though is very much dependent not only upon investment, but on research and development funding that creates innovation in key sectors of national infrastructure and is also key to maintaining a buoyant manufacturing sector. Below I look at three key areas of UK infrastructure to highlight the paucity of our current situation: transport, housing and energy.

Transport

Whereas countries like France and Spain have high speed rail networks, the UK is behind schedule and over budget on building one relatively short high speed rail line. Such is the controversy, there are even mutterings of abandoning the project. In France high speed rail has been a reality since the early 1980s, and in China bullet trains now reach speeds of over 200mph making the 800 mile trip between Shanghai and Beijing in under four hours. China (like some other nations) is also investing in the next evolution of high speed rail: magnetic levitation. These trains are already operational on some lines and reaching speeds of 268mph.[11]

Despite lacking any such innovation on our railways, the UK has the most expensive rail fares in Europe, according to passenger watchdog Passenger Focus, with some commuters paying more than four times the amount for comparable journeys elsewhere in Europe. The problem is what *The Guardian* economics correspondent Aditya Chakrabortty calls "legalised larceny". He's not wrong, according to research, UK train companies gained an average return of 147% on every pound they put into their business.[12] The UK's rail services, like so many other privatised industries, are decreasingly run to serve the public, and increasingly to extract the maximum possible return for private shareholders. But at the same time as charging the most expensive fares, the UK's privatised railways remain massively subsidised by the government, with state subsidy higher today than under the nationalised British Rail.

It is perhaps unsurprising that the UK public remains committed to renationalisation of the railways, with opinion polls consistently showing between two-thirds and three-quarters in favour.

There are also good environmental reasons in favour of increasing rail capacity in that it shifts travellers away from more polluting road and air transport. This is known in the industry as encouraging modal shift. The potential is evident from the story of the Paris to Marseille transport route. Rail held only 22% of the combined Paris-Marseille air-rail market before TGV Mediterranean went into service in 2001, but within five years it was 69%, meaning considerably less air pollution.

With the ongoing debate about UK airport capacity, the missing piece is the role of government to consider alternatives on the basis of social and environmental considerations. The airline industry has no interest in so doing, and that is why it is essential that government plays its role, acting in the public interest.

Energy

Like the railways, the UK's energy industries have also been and remain privatised. Despite opinion polling showing

Renewable energy use as a % of total energy use, 2013

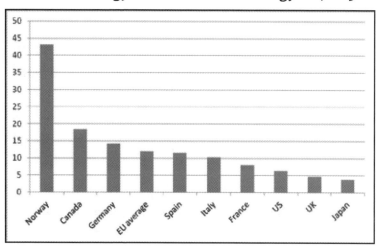

Source: Enerdata[14]

over two-thirds of the UK public believing energy should be renationalised,[13] no political party has even hinted at the prospect. The public attachment to public ownership is not sentimentalism but both economically and environmentally rational. UK energy prices have increased markedly in recent years, and the UK's energy supply remains heavily dependent on fossil fuels. The privatised and deregulated energy companies have failed to invest in renewables, and the government has sat idly by too. If you compare UK energy consumption from renewable to comparable countries, the UK's position is a poor indictment (see above).

The UK's consumption of renewable energy lags far behind other major European economies, and across the EU as a whole renewable energy consumption is three times the UK level as a proportion of total energy use. If you compare the UK with the other North Sea oil rich nation of Norway, the contrast is even more stark.

Some argue that nuclear power provides an alternative future away from fossil fuels, but increasingly nations are turning their back on the non-renewable fuel that leaves a lasting expensive legacy, with the public cost of disposing of the UK's nuclear waste estimated by the National Audit Office to be £67.5 billion. According to the Public Accounts Committee in the House of Commons, "there's no indication of when that cost will stop rising". And, as the Fukushima plant disaster in Japan showed, nuclear power remains a potent risk even in operation. Germany is currently committed to scrapping its nuclear capacity in full by 2022, while Japan is greatly reducing its nuclear reliance. Many countries, including Italy, have no nuclear capacity. Nevertheless, in 2013 the coalition government signed contracts with foreign companies to build a new generation of nuclear power stations, at a guaranteed price of £92.50 per megawatt hour of electricity, rising in line with inflation, for the first thirty-five years of its operation. That price is almost twice the current wholesale price of electricity when the deal was signed in 2013, and so it guarantees UK energy bills will continue to rise considerably. The government will also subsidise the construction of the plants. The companies involved are nationalised French and Chinese corporations, yet no political party in the UK will countenance UK public ownership of our energy infrastructure. This is the price that the UK is paying for thirty years of the government leaving our energy supply to private interests.

Even if you are sceptical about the necessity to change for environmental reasons – though denying man-made climate change is as rational as believing the Earth to be flat – the reality is that fossil and nuclear fuels are depleting. As they become more scarce their price will rise. So there are economic and environmental reasons to switch to renewables.

Housing

UK housing is another deeply problematic sector, with the major problem being the lack of investment in new housing stock. The UK has a significant housing shortage, which has kept UK housing expensive and on a rising curve. The increasing demand and lack of supply leads to rising prices. In the mid-1990s the average UK home was worth 80% of the average US home. By 2012, the average UK home was worth nearly 200% of the average in the US.[15] In the ten years between 2001 and 2011, UK house prices rose a staggering 94% while wages rose only by 29%, according to the National Housing Federation.

The failure of successive governments to build sufficient housing has kept increasing numbers of UK families locked out of the housing market and concentrates housing in the hands of those rich enough to buy more. Access to housing has been significantly constrained by the selling off of council housing, and the cap on council borrowing which has prevented councils replacing it. Over two million households are now on housing waiting lists, and across the capital an astonishing 1 in 10 Londoners are on council waiting lists. Housing has become a profitable investment for a new class of landlords, whose unrestrained rents means their tenants are unable to save enough to buy a home themselves. As a result there is a growing housing apartheid in the UK, which causes disruption to the increased number of families forced to live in temporary and overcrowded accommodation.

Even for those able to buy, surveys show that the size of the average family home has reduced, as has the size of gardens. Generations who seek to own their own home today are also paying more in mortgage payments for longer for more cramped conditions. About 20% of mortgages now are to repaid over terms of 30 years or more.[16] In 2013 the ONS found that for the first time since the end of the second world war the proportion of people who own their own home declined, back to levels last seen in 1987. Similarly, another government survey found that, for the first time on record, more people were renting privately from landlords than from a council or housing association.[17] Even since the passing of direct buy-to-let mortgage tax breaks, the Intergenerational Foundation found that UK taxpayers provide a £5 billion annual subsidy for buy-to-let landlords, through favourable taxation arrangements.[18]

Our ageing housing infrastructure means higher energy bills for those who live in older housing stock, and most tragically a higher proportion of excess winter deaths as the UK's older homes are poorly insulated. Although various government and council schemes have reduced the problem, it is now possible to build housing (especially as a part of a new development or new town) that is virtually self-sufficient in its energy needs, yet the government has not dared impose such regulations on new build housing or to invest in building new high quality housing itself.

Housing policy fulfils one of the most basic human needs, for shelter. With the technology we have available we can aspire to more than simply shelter, but innovation that brings social and environmental benefits. Sadly though, housing policy has been largely outsourced to property developers and land speculators.

The failure of the labour market

While the finance sector, centred in and around the City of London's square mile, has a perverse effect on the London housing market, its ability to suck UK capital from elsewhere depresses industry in other parts of the country.

So another consequence of the UK failing to invest productively is that it produces fewer good jobs and average wages fall and unemployment rises. Since the onset of recession in 2008 to 2012, the real value of wages in the UK has fallen by 7% (equating to a collective loss of £50 billion a year to all UK workers). During the same period there has been a real terms drop in consumer demand of 5%,[19] damaging the retail sector and creating economic risk through increased debt levels. With the cost of living rising as real wages fall, people are forced to take on debt to makes ends meet or to cut back on their spending as more of their income is spent servicing debt repayments. Either option further inflates the relative size of the UK financial sector, by restricting growth in other sectors and by increasing the demand for consumer credit. In 2013 UK households remained deeper in debt than those in either the US, Germany or France.

The link between declining real wages and trade union membership cannot be ignored. In the late 1970s, over 12 million workers were members of trade unions, today the figure is only half that, and the workforce is larger today. As a result, whereas 85% of workers were covered by collective bargaining agreements (meaning pay is negotiated between the employer and a trade union) in 1979, fewer than 40% are today. The consequence is clear in terms of falling real wages, so the share of the national income going to workers as wages has fallen from around 60% in the 1960s and 70s to only 55% today.[20]

But the declining strength of workers and their unions in the workplace does not tell the whole story. Research by Professor Alan Felstead at Cardiff University found that in 2006 there was an oversupply of labour for qualified workers (whether with GSCEs or graduate level qualifications). The UK labour market shortage was actually for people with no qualifications. In other words the UK was creating jobs for people with no qualifications, and was unable to find work that matched the qualifications of its highly skilled workforce. The failure to have any government strategy meant UK workers' skills were not being utilised at work – wasting talent and productive capacity.

Without any industrial strategy outside of prostration to the demands of the finance sector, the UK has increasingly become a low wage economy. This view is shared by the head of the Federation of European Employers, Robin Chater, who doesn't mince his words:

> "The UK is turning into an old-style third world country with low pay growth for most workers below managerial level, widening pay differentials and poor levels of capital investment." [21]

In the late 1970s only around 12% of workers earned less than two-thirds of the average wage. By the mid-1980s that had risen to around 17% of workers being low paid. Today the figure is around 22%.[22] Compared to the rest of the world, only the US has higher levels of low wage work. France, Finland, Norway, Italy and Belgium all have less than half the rate of low wage work of the UK.[23]

Work has also become increasingly precarious for many: a succession of temporary contracts or the uncertainty of zero hours contracts. For up to a million people at work on zero hours contracts, they awake on a Monday morning with no guarantee whether they will be working today or this week. Under such circumstances planning finances, childcare, claiming your entitled tax credits, or just organising your life becomes a matter of supreme complexity. Even many of those with regular hours are blighted by low pay. The national minimum wage, introduced in the first term of Tony Blair's government put a floor under exploitative pay levels, but was set and remains too low. In 2011, the UK minimum wage was worth only 35% of the average wage, in Belgium it is 40%, Canada 44%, France 46% and in New Zealand 54%.[24] When Tony Blair boasted that the UK had "the most flexible labour market in Europe", it meant UK workers had the fewest protections, least rights and most restrictive anti-union laws. Just as coalition government chancellor Osborne boasted about how the UK charged the lowest taxes, Blair advertised the UK by offering the country's workers as the most exploitable.

Raising wages and reducing inequality is not just about paying people more for the work they do, but about directing investment to create jobs in industries that can utilise the UK's currently underutilised workforce. We have a wealth of untapped human potential in our economy, and as the section above on infrastructure shows, no shortage of need for skilled workers.

A social failure: inequality

Inequality is more often perceived as a moral or social problem than an economic problem. There are indeed sound moral arguments against the level of inequality that exists in the UK today. It would, on a moral basis, be simple to make the case that the current level of UK inequality is unjustifiable. However, the level of UK inequality is also an economic reality, and that reality needs to be changed for economic reasons too. In other words, reducing inequality isn't just about making us feel better or assuaging our guilt, it is in our collective economic interest to be more equal.

We live in a deeply unequal society. While increasing numbers of people in the UK live in poverty, at the other end of the scale the wealth of the elite continues to grow. The 2012 Sunday Times Rich List revealed that the richest 1,000 Britons increased their wealth by £35 billion in the last year. Contrastingly, between 2010 and 2012 an extra million UK people fell into poverty – including an extra 300,000 children. In 2013, the average annual pay rise among UK workers slipped to below 1%, the pay package of directors of the UK's largest companies rose by 14%. The Institute for Fiscal Studies, an independent thinktank estimated in June 2013 that "median net incomes will be no higher in 2015/16 than they were in 2002/03".[25] In contrast, in Tony Blair's years as prime minister the incomes of the richest 0.1% increased by 83%, compared to just 18% for the bottom 90% (i.e. the overwhelming majority).[26]

The UK is abnormal in this regard. The income and consumption of our wealthiest 10% is 13.8 times that of the bottom 10%. In France that ratio is 9.1 times, in Germany only 6.9 times, in Finland 5.6 times, and in Japan just 4.5 times. Only Singapore, the US and Portugal have greater inequality than the UK.[27]

As we saw in chapter 3, the better off now pay proportionately less tax than the less well-off – and that's before factoring in tax avoidance by the super-rich. With ever more income and relatively less tax levied, the very richest are accumulating ever more wealth.

Income and wealth operate similarly to deficit and debt. The gap between your income and what you spend is a deficit – a gap that needs to be filled – that gap builds debt and it rises over time unless the deficit closes. The same is true of income and wealth. The more surplus income you have (over and above the money you spend) accumulates as wealth. This may manifest itself as money in the bank, housing, fine art, wine or antiques, etc. For three generations now, the expectation of many people in the UK has been that they would accumulate over the course of their lives enough to allow them to eventually own a home, and have some modest savings, which bolstered by the basic state pension would allow them security and dignity in retirement.

The accumulation of wealth makes a mockery of those economists who predicted wealth would trickle down. It hasn't. It has been sucked up in a vacuum effect. The US economic commentator Robert Reich has coined the phrase 'trickle-up economics' to describe the same phenomenon. It is somewhat like in the board game Monopoly in which one player ends up with all the money and all the property, while everyone else goes bankrupt. The popular family board game was created to show how rents enriched property owners and impoverished tenants and was originally called 'The Landlord's Game'. Although everybody starts off with equal money and no property, through nothing more than sheer luck (roll of the dice) one player accumulates all of the wealth. It is not too far removed from what would happen in our economy if the ameliorating effects of taxation, public services and social security were removed. However, while the player who successfully bankrupts their opposing players at the end of the game is the winner, in reality the economy doesn't end at any point. Large inequalities do however leave many struggling to survive. The knock-on effects of eroding consumer spending power spells economic disaster, since the companies' goods and services, landlords' rents, and banks' debt repayments become unaffordable. It is in this way that US banks crashed, as those with sub-prime mortgages could no longer make the repayments, as we saw in chapter 1.

For private equity billionaires life must be like a game of Monopoly. These unaccountable mega-rich have used their wealth to buy entire companies (including well-known companies like the AA, Birds Eye, Boots, Dr Martens, Hertz, and Hilton hotels). Private equity companies have reaped huge profits by cutting jobs, selling off sites, downgrading or closing workers' pension schemes, relocating head offices to tax havens, and have sometimes left the companies loaded with colossal debts, before selling them on.

Inequality means while some can afford to take early retirement, pension age rises mean increasingly working longer for the rest. For the majority of those starting out at work today retirement cannot be expected before 70 years old. It is unclear how those doing manual jobs will be able to continue to work into their old age. The reality is that for many the future is working for longer and dying sooner in their retirement, while for the rich who can afford early retirement the future is a longer retirement. Increasing the state pension age only affects those without the assets and savings to enable early retirement. The only prize for living longer for many – achieved collectively through publicly funded medical advances and improved healthcare – will be to work longer.

The wealthy wield considerable power over our lives, determining: what goods and services we can buy and how much we pay for them; where, whether, how and for how long we work; and shaping our media through direct ownership and the purchase of advertising space. These people are frequently lauded as 'wealth creators', but in reality they are merely wealth hoarders. In 2005 it was estimated that wealthy individuals held a quarter of all global wealth ($11.5 trillion) offshore, avoiding $250 billion in tax every year. It is hard to comprehend what even that smaller latter figure of $250 billion means in real terms, but for comparative purposes it is two to three times as much as the annual global aid budget to relieve poverty in developing countries.[28]

The UK has not been so unequal since the 1930s, at the time George Orwell was documenting England's brutal poverty while writing *The Road to Wigan Pier*.[29] The economic inequality of today likewise lacks any justification. People's wages bear no relation to their contribution to society – a nurse earns in a year what a Premier League footballer earns in one day. A care worker for the elderly or severely disabled earns perhaps £16,000 a year – just 1/1000th of the pay of the chief executive of fashion company Burberry, who walked away with £16 million in 2013.

Our society is organised so that anyone who is unemployed, unable to work due to sickness or disability, or relies on the basic state pension is condemned to poverty. The basic state pension has declined in value to just 15% of average male earnings, down from 25% thirty-five years ago, while unemployment benefit was worth 28% of average earnings in 1967. By the time Thatcher left office it was only 18%, and by 2013 it had fallen to just 13%. As union representation in the workplace has declined, so has the number of private sector employees in defined benefit pension schemes[30] has fallen from 34% in 1997 to 11% in 2010. Over the same time period, the proportion of private sector workers in any occupational scheme fell from about half in 1997 to just one-third by 2010.[31] These cuts in workers' pension provision was motivated by profit, reducing the benefits on offer to workers to maximise profits to business owners.

Living on a financial knife-edge many households struggle to make ends meet – the money runs out by the end of the month and they are forced into desperate economising or into the hands of money-lenders. Inevitably many fall into arrears, failing to pay bills and facing the harassment of red notices and, ultimately, bailiffs and county court, exacerbating their deprivation.

For those who live in private rented accommodation or who are struggling to meet mortgage payments they fight a monthly battle to keep their home – with eviction notices and repossession orders a constant worry. In January 2014, the homelessness charity Shelter reported that household budgets were "at breaking point", with one in 11 people worried they will not be able to afford their rent or mortgage that month.[32] For those who have already lost a home or are unable to afford one, the overcrowding, indignity and regular upheaval of temporary accommodation is even worse.

The concentration of economic power gives a few people great power over the lives of others. Those who own excess properties are able to raise rents or evict tenants at short notice – without having to take any consideration of the effect of those decisions on their tenants.

In 2013, rents in London rose by 4.8% – after years of above inflation rises. London's housing market is affected by the financialisation of the UK economy in other ways too. The status of the City of London as an effective tax haven attracts wealthy people from across the world, keen to take up residence and take advantage of non-domicile status to avoid tax. This has in turn inflated house prices, initially in the most salubrious areas like Mayfair and Hampstead, but with knock-on effects throughout the city. The rapidly rising house prices and favourable tax laws make London housing (in particular) an attractive investment opportunity for the globe's wealthy elite.

In half of all London's boroughs, the average cost of renting a one bedroom flat is more than the total annual earnings of someone working full-time on the minimum wage. London politicians, from left-wing Islington Labour MP Jeremy Corbyn to right-wing Conservative London Mayor Boris Johnson, have expressed concern about "social cleansing" of the capital as the low paid are forced out.

It costs us all too – not just those of us who rent privately. For those on low pay or on out of work benefits, housing benefit enables around five million households to keep a roof over their heads. Total housing benefit spending has ballooned to £24 billion a year. While only 33% of people who claim housing benefit live in private accommodation, 68% of the most expensive housing claims come from those renting privately. In recent years, the majority of new housing benefit claims have come from working households, as wages are unable to meet the rising cost of rents.

Those who employ staff are able to make them redundant at short notice, reduce their hours or their pay. In large companies, the interests of a few people or even just one person can affect thousands of workers and entire communities. This was abundantly clear in the case of the oil refinery at Grangemouth in Scotland. The refinery provided 85% of Scotland's petrol, and much to Northern Ireland and northern England too. But billionaire owner Jim Ratcliffe threatened to shutdown the site unless workers accepted lower wages, an end to final salary pensions, accepted union officials being barred from the site, and no right to strike for three years. The workers and their union appealed to both the UK and Scottish governments, but ultimately it was a privately owned business and the owner could do what he wanted.

Being rich also gives the super-wealthy access to politicians that is unattainable to the rest of the public. Money is power – and a deeply anti-democratic power at that. The House of Lords is populated by many who have been major donors to the UK political parties. The cash for peerages scandal in 2006 and 2007 showed that an unlikely proportion of Labour Party donors were being nominated for seats in the House of Lords. Similarly, within the first year of the coalition government taking office, the Prime Minister was accused of using Downing Street to solicit party donations, from a succession of private dinners with millionaires.

The phone hacking scandal exposed not only the inhumanity of hacking into the phones of murdered children or grieving relatives. It also exposed the subservience of the politicians of all the major political parties to newspaper proprietors, and the tight social networks that existed between editors, senior politicians and senior police officers.

The UK likes to believe it has a free press. It has no such thing. Much of our print media is heavily subsidised by unaccountable multi-millionaire owners. As such the 'news' is refracted through the biases of those owners. Even after the closure of the News of the World in the aftermath of the phone hacking scandal, its owners – Rupert Murdoch's News International – still retained 34% of the UK newspaper circulation.

As Harriet Harman QC MP said in the wake of the Leveson inquiry:

> "Media monopoly matters in a democracy. The concentration of unaccountable media power distorts the political system. The media shapes how we see ourselves and how we see the world. In a democracy, the free flow of information, of different points of view, is crucial for open debate.
>
> "Too much power in too few hands hinders proper debate. Plurality ensures that no media owner can exert such a damaging influence on public opinion and on policy makers." [33]

Conclusion

Countries that have weak and incompetent leadership, high levels of institutionalised corruption, little protection for the citizens, and where wealth and power are concentrated in the hands of an unaccountable few, are commonly referred to as failed states. The UK has a failed economy.

The politicians that led us into the financial crisis did not understand the economy they oversaw, and the politicians post-crisis have no answers except to carry on as before in the vain hope that somehow it will work the second time around. They are competing to manage a failed experiment.

That our economy has failed is not predominantly an economic failure, it is a political failure – a failure of democracy. The UK economy moulded by successive generations of politicians has become progressively less and less guided by democratic decisions and more and more guided by decisions of what makes a short-term profit, in the interests of a wealthy elite.

Greed is not good. And neither is profit. The UK has developed a social and economic culture in which selfishness (often disguised by euphemisms such as 'individualism' or 'wealth creation') has become lauded. Instead of deference to hereditary power, we are now invited to show our admiration and awe for the rich. To give this farce a facade of credibility, we are told the rich are 'entreprenuers', 'successful businessmen' (they are mostly men) or, most hubristically of all, 'wealth creators'. We must do what is in their interests for without their goodwill and wise counsel we shall all surely perish.

It is this belief that has guided successive generations of politicians. From Thatcher's influential chancellor Nigel Lawson building a "pro-profit, pro-business" culture, to New Labour guru Peter Mandelson reassuring the City that the newly elected Labour government was "intensely relaxed about people getting filthy rich".[34] Today the Conservative Mayor of London, Boris Johnson praises "the spirit of envy and keeping up with the Joneses that is, like greed, a valuable spur to economic activity".

These same politicians have backed up these words with deeds too. George Osborne, the chancellor in the coalition government of David Cameron, reduced corporation tax dramatically hailing "a headline rate that is not just lower than our competitors, but dramatically lower ... an advertisement for investment and jobs in Britain".[35] In doing so he was following in the footsteps of his predecessors. From Geoffrey Howe under Thatcher to Alistair Darling under Gordon Brown corporation tax was cut from 52% in 1979 to just 28%, even before Osborne entered 11 Downing Street. So let the rich keep more and they will flood to Britain bringing jobs and wealth for all. This is the flawed logic of those who believe the only or at least prime motivation in life is personal enrichment. Their logic suggests that for most selfish of motives the most collectively beneficial outcome can be achieved. That really is as stupid as it sounds.

Francis Maude, a minister in the governments of Thatcher, Major and Cameron, and a former investment banker, said it was "a compliment" for the UK to be described as a tax haven, and added: "That is exactly what we are trying to do".[36] While the UK economy has increasingly come to cannibalise itself, it now also sees its remaining main role in sucking resources from other nations in a parasitic relationship, as a tax haven.

So besotted are recent generations of politicians with the wealthy that they have sought to bring their 'talents' into government, without any notable successes. In 2006, when New Labour wanted to appoint someone to review UK social security policy, it appointed investment banker David Freud – who confessed he "didn't know anything about welfare at all". Nevertheless, his report that described welfare as "a multi-billion industry" shaped Labour's welfare policy. In 2009 he defected to the Tories who ennobled him. Baron Freud became the Coalition Government's Welfare Minister, and the dweller in an 8-bedroom central London mansion was apparently responsible for the imposition of the bedroom tax – punishing people in social housing for the failure of successive government to ensure sufficient housing. This ugly episode perhaps illustrates best the interchangeability between the two major governing parties from their welfare policies to their adoration of the finance sector. According to *The Guardian* newspaper, the Labour government of Blair and Brown gave honours to 23 bankers, four of whom received life peerages, and seven were knighted. Three were made government ministers, two appointed to senior posts within Downing Street, ten were placed on eminent councils, seven on agencies and quangos, while 37 were drafted in to head up taskforces, or sit on commissions and advisory bodies.[37]

The banking crash did little to change this trend. The coalition government under David Cameron decided shortly after its election that it should review government efficiency. It chose billionaire tax dodger Sir Philip Green to lead the review. Green, who runs the Arcadia group of retail companies, bought it in 2002, but sold it to Tina Green, his wife, within 24 hours. His wife is a Monaco resident and the company paid out £1.2 billion in dividends – £285 million of which would have been liable to tax had the owner been UK resident. Unsurprisingly, he made no recommendations on improving the government's efficiency in clamping down on tax avoidance.

Another Cameron-era appointee was Stephen Green, who was ennobled to become Baron Green of Hurstpierpoint and was appointed minister for trade and investment. Green was chairman of the HSBC bank at the time of its $2 billion fine for money laundering and sanctions-busting in the US (see chapter 3). His successor as HSBC chairman was Stuart Gulliver, who commented "between 2004 and 2010 [when Green was at the helm], our anti-money laundering controls should have been stronger and more effective and we failed to spot and deal with unacceptable behaviour"[38] – quite an endorsement for someone to be put in charge of UK trade and investment policy.

The above is not designed to be an exhaustive account of bankers and business executives in government. But the appointment of individuals to positions of responsibility, with seemingly their only qualifying criteria being that they are wealthy, is indicative of the culture that developed in UK politics in which economic policy was not about building a good standard of living for all, but in which government had outsourced economic policy to finance capital – and even insourced figures from finance capital to run government.

The priorities for the finance sector, and the super-rich, are in direct conflict with the democratic aims of operating an economy in the public interest.

Even following the collapse of their economic model with the finance sector crash, no major political party offered any industrial vision. As the BBC's business editor, Robert Peston concluded in October 2013:

> "The government has more-or-less given up on a fundamental rebalancing and reconstruction of the British economy away from banking ... the Establishment has returned to the comforting conviction that the City is golden-egg laying goose, and not a Trojan horse".

Without any challenge to this view, the finance sector's dominance will continue, the UK's creaking infrastructure fails to receive the necessary investment, any industrial recovery will remain a pipedream, and our society will remain deeply unequal. In short unless the finance sector beast is caged, it will continue its marauding and trail of carnage.

Our current economic model needs to be overthrown, just as peoples around the world have overthrown the corrupt regimes of monarchy and tinpot dictatorship. We need a revolutionary and emancipatory change to build an economy as if people mattered.

Just as the Chartists, Suffragettes and trade unionists fought for political democracy in the nineteenth and early twentieth centuries, so today we need comparable social movements to democratise the economy, money and wealth.

In the final chapter, I propose some democratic economic policies that politicians might propose if they were committed to running the economy in the public interest, as if people mattered.

5
Building an economy that works

Having come this far – after tens of thousands of words and a year[1] of researching and writing – the temptation is to stop and make this book purely about explaining the crash and the challenges the UK economy faces. That would certainly be the easier option, but it would feel like a cop out. Having criticised successive governments for abdicating their responsibilities it would be hypocritical to not put forward a better way of running the economy as if people mattered.

As that great analyst of capitalism Karl Marx said, "the philosophers have only interpreted the world, the point however is to change it". And so this final chapter addresses the challenge of making the UK economy work in the collective interest, as if we, the people, were of prime importance.

Throughout this book the point has been to show that the economic problems we face were directly or indirectly the consequence of political decisions. In the UK successive governments have diminished their own role in economic policy leaving a void filled by various private companies and super-rich individuals inevitably acting in their own interests, regardless of what may be in the public interest.

And when the government was forced to intervene in the economy – in the aftermath of the biggest banking crisis in UK history – it bailed out the banks, but not UK citizens whose homes were being repossessed, who were losing their jobs, and who were going bankrupt or being declared insolvent. In contrast the Icelandic government, whose banks were also hit hard during the crisis, announced a 150 billion kronur scheme to bail out its mortgage holders. At 9% of Icelandic GDP, the equivalent would be £133 billion of aid to UK mortgage holders.

So we need to democratise our economy. There are two key criteria for democracy: firstly that people have the power to change things; and secondly that people have as equal as possible power to change things. "Democracy transferred power from the wallet to the ballot", as Tony Benn argued. His quip neatly encompasses the inherent linkage between politics and economics. Before universal suffrage people couldn't afford to buy education or healthcare, but once they had political power, they could vote for it instead.

Today we need to strengthen that conception. If we want an economy that operates in the public interest, we need to curtail private power. Just as democracy and universal suffrage brought political rights (e.g. to vote, to stand for election, to form a political party) we now need democratic economic rights.

Public ownership

You can't control what you don't own, so the private ownership of public goods needs to be ended so that key parts of our economy are democratically controlled and accountable.

If you privatise public infrastructure and services, you end up privatising the public interest too. Governments sold off public assets and with it the public stake in the economy. What's good for those industries became what is good for private interests. The simple reality is that no one would have been interested in buying the assets like the bus companies or Royal Mail unless the service was significantly deregulated too. That is the only way that a profit margin can be achieved.

In 1945, a Labour government was elected to power in a landslide victory. After the horrors of the second world war, it faced a public debt around four times larger than that which confronted the coalition government in 2010. It nationalised industries including coal, steel, rail, road haulage, civil aviation, electricity and gas. How did it do it? Surely the second world war had "maxed out the nation's credit card", as David Cameron would put it sixty-five years later. Clement Attlee's Labour government did what the banks do. It created the money (but through government bonds). It exchanged government bonds to the value of the shares in the industries, and compulsorily purchased them.

Governments from Thatcher to Cameron have emphasised the need for more entrepreneurialism and dynamism in the economy. Yet paradoxically they have privatised any role for the state they were running to be either of those things. UK governments from 1979 onwards have shied away from running anything in an entrepreneurial way. The very people advocating this entrepreneurial culture have been the ones pushing any entrepreneurial activity away from themselves. It would be a fair criticism of the nationalised industries of that era to say they were not always at the cutting edge of dynamism, although they often acted incredibly resourcefully to provide universal services on a shoestring.

So a government acting in the public interest should invest and be entrepreneurial. The current level of political and economic debate is so dire that this will immediately be met with cries of 'more borrowing' or 'burdening future generations with debt'. Borrowing is not a bad thing in itself and can create assets rather than burdens. There are essentially two types of borrowing. There is the borrowing that governments, businesses and households do when struggling to make ends meet. This crisis management may be necessary in some circumstances but it is neither ideal nor sustainable. Then there is borrowing to invest, which brings a return. Many households borrow to buy a house. This is a sound investment, and most often a sustainable debt which in the long-term will reduce outgoings and act as a buffer against future hardship.

As noted in chapter four the UK has chronic underinvestment in housing, renewable energy and transport networks. Investing in projects to build a million new council homes, to greatly expand our energy supply from renewable energy – up to and beyond the current European average – and to build a high speed rail network would cost tens of billions of pounds. Such spending produces a return. The tenants of council housing will pay rents (and there is the added saving of lower housing benefit payments and expenditure on temporary accommodation). Households and businesses will pay for their energy use through their bills, and rail passengers will pay fares. This is before it is calculated that the construction of such infrastructure creates employment, bringing tax revenues to government and savings on social security expenditure, as well as generating economic activity in supply chains throughout the economy.

This Land is Your Land

Half a generation ago, the Ramblers and other campaigners won the 'right to roam'. It opened up rights for all of us to enjoy the countryside. According to the Ramblers, whereas before only 4% of the Yorkshire dales was accessible to the public, today it is 64%, as is 85% of the Northumberland national park from only 19% before the Countryside and Rights of Way Act was passed in 2000. The US folk singer Woody Guthrie would have been proud. His most famous song is 'This land is your land', but rather less well-known is the rebellious ending:

"As I went walking I saw a sign there
And on the sign it said 'private property',
But on the back side it didn't say nothing.
That side was made for you and me."

The land was here before we were born and it will be here after we are long since departed. Does this mean all land should be publicly owned? Perhaps. The key question though is whether we should all have a democratic say over what use the land around us is put to. In the UK today, over two-thirds of the land is owned by just 0.3% of people.[2] Ownership of the land is rather ridiculous. As Dave Wetzel, an advocate of land value tax, says:

"For most of the hundred thousand years of humankind's existence on this planet, land has been shared as a common resource like the air we breathe, the wind that turns windmills or the sunshine we rely upon to grow our crops and provide us with energy and good health".[3]

Since the value of the land is created collectively, through mostly public investment in roads, pavements, street lights, nearby social amenities and infrastructure, advocates of a land value tax suggest that the resultant land values should be collectively captured through an annual tax set at a small proportion of its value (rates ranging from 0.1% to 1% have been suggested) depending on the land use (e.g. housing, retail, agriculture or industry). For individuals, the tax could be deferred until death – making it an effective inheritance tax – and a personal allowance could be permitted (e.g. land necessary for an average home plot) in a similar way to the personal allowance on income tax. A land value tax has many attractions, not least that it is much harder to hide land than it is money. Land cannot be hidden in offshore tax havens. It also addresses wealth inequality – the result of accumulated income inequality and could help to stabilise house prices, and therefore stabilise home life for many families in the UK. It could of course also be tax neutral, rather than an additional tax, either through offsetting against existing taxes, or by replacing taxes such as council tax, business rates and others. Another benefit is that it encourages landowners to bring land into use, as the necessity of paying land value tax means there is a financial penalty on developers buying land and waiting for values to increase, in the mean time restricting supply. A land value tax therefore further stabilises property prices by deterring land speculation.[4]

Taxing the land is therefore effective at tackling wealth inequalities and ensuring more productive use of land (and therefore generating economic growth) – as well as being morally just.

Taming the global financial system

The growth of the finance sector, most markedly in the UK which has the largest finance sector of any major economy, is a reflection of global wealth inequalities and the economic power that can be wielded by a few. Taming the global financial system is therefore an essential prerequisite of building a more stable economy which acts in the public interest.

Advocates of the current arrangements of the global financial system would say that it has brought unparalleled global prosperity. They would be mistaken. As economists Arvind Subramanian and Dani Rodrik have shown, "financial globalisation has not generated increased investment or higher growth ... countries that have grown most rapidly have been those that rely least on capital inflows".[5]

In sucking in capital from around the world the UK has an inflated finance sector. When the banking system crashed, the

UK's bloated finance sector was bailed out as too big to fail, placing an enormous burden on the UK government and us all as taxpayers. The golden goose became a giant albatross around our necks – deepening the recession, delaying any economic recovery, and leading to huge cuts in public services as government sought to cut its costs.

There is a reason why banks locate their head offices in the nations with the largest economies rather than in tax havens. It is because they need the political power to lobby on their behalf in the global arena, and the economic capacity to bail them out should they get into trouble. Banks may set up subsidiaries in tax havens to avoid paying their dues, but their head offices are always proudly located in the major cities of the major economies. In doing so, they effectively nationalise their risk and offshore their profits.

The first thing to do therefore must be to nationalise the banks. As I wrote in chapter one:

> "The banks hold our cash, they hold our savings, they have our mortgages, and the wider finance sector invests our pension funds. Our bills are paid by direct debits, our shopping is paid for using debit or credit cards, our wages and benefits are transferred into our accounts. The system is vital".

It is simply too important to fail. Just as government cannot shrug its shoulders when rail companies fail (as they did on the east coast mainline in 2009) when banks fail government has to step in. But while that's the negative case 'too important to fail', there is also a positive case.

The post-war Labour government nationalised the Bank of England in 1946 (before then it was an independent private institution founded in 1694). However, the post-war Labour government had little vision for the Bank of England and it remained largely unchanged, but it should have a new role as an public investment bank with a remit set by parliament, under democratic control. At the moment, the Bank of England's primary mandate is to maintain inflation at around 2%.[6] A new expanded mandate, set by parliament, could focus on creating full employment.

The Bank of England could also offer finance to public institutions for investment. It could do so at cheaper rates than those charged through the PFI schemes by profiteering companies, and in a similar way to the Bank of England's Special Liquidity Scheme or Bank Recapitalisation fund used to bail out the banking system – using a hypothecated fund to channel investment into the UK's energy, housing and transport infrastructure. It should also fund research and development, where again the UK lags similar major economies. This would be far more beneficial to an economy run in the public interest than the hundreds of billions used for quantitative easing (see chapter one).

The UK consumer has been ripped off by the banks too. Following the crash, UK banks widened their margins between the interest they pay to savers and the interest they charge borrowers. This was rapacious profiteering (in 2012 UK bank margins were 296 basis points compared with 160 basis points across the Eurozone countries).[7] In the aftermath of the nationalisation of Northern Rock, CBI director general Richard Lambert, said: "It is critically important that state ownership of the bank should not be allowed to distort the savings market, through access to government funds on favourable terms". This roughly translates as a publicly-owned bank can offer better terms to savers ("distort the savings market" in CBI-speak), and in 2008 the *Daily Mail* reported that "rival banks protested that the nationalised company could enjoy a huge competitive advantage over them and steal business away". So if a publicly owned bank could offer better terms to consumers why on earth shouldn't one exist? It should. And it would in an economy run in the public interest. One option would be to nationalise the entire high street banking sector (through swapping Treasury bonds for shares), which seems far easier than the alternative of setting up a national bank chain that slowly did, as the private profiteers fear, undercut the private banks and put them out of business.

By offering lower interest rates to borrowers, and potentially higher rates to savers a public banking system could reduce the risks of debt crises. By strategically investing in key sectors, the banking system could also play a leading role in tackling unemployment (especially in regions of high unemployment) and rebuilding our infrastructure – supporting industry and people.

The UK must also take on its tax havens – the crown dependencies like Jersey and the Cayman Islands. They are the arteries of the global tax avoidance system. These corrupt island nations could be stopped by the UK, their sponsor, at any point. But they play a pivotal role within the global financial system. The UK bank Barclays lists 120 subsidiary companies in the Cayman Islands alone. In May 2013, the anti-poverty charity ActionAid found that only two of the UK's largest 100 companies had no subsidiaries in tax havens. Between these 98 companies, there were 1,685 subsidiaries in tax havens that were either UK crown dependencies or overseas territories like Gibraltar and Bermuda. The government could stop this abuse overnight, if it wanted to. The UK provides military protection to these nations, yet their contribution is to help undermine the UK's tax revenue that supports their own protection. But this assumes that governments serve in the public interest, they don't. It is very useful for big business, and especially big finance, to keep some of their affairs offshore and beyond scrutiny, or taxation. In China, Hong Kong operates as a similarly corrupt quasi-independent outlet. Such tax havens, or secrecy jurisdictions as the Tax Justice Network describes them, are not only bad for the loss of tax revenues, but they shield from public scrutiny a whole range of criminal activity from terrorism[8] to people and drug trafficking.

At the centre of this web of tax havens is the City of London, constitutionally a quasi-independent city state, where only some legislation passed by the UK government applies (e.g. the Freedom of Information Act only applies in part). The Corporation of London runs the affairs of the City and acts as the primary global lobbyist on behalf of the finance sector and its own freedoms (from democracy and public scrutiny). It is not democratically elected but a labyrinthine maze of sheriffs, aldermen, livery companies and a lord mayor. If that sounds like something reminiscent of the medieval era, that's because it is. Businesses have votes in the elections, weighted to their number of employees – and the votes are cast as a block (the employees don't even know the votes are being cast), meaning businesses get 32,000 votes while the 9,000 residents get the usual one vote each. The City of London has been described as our "last rotten borough" by Labour MP John McDonnell. Former Labour minister Tony Benn said it was "an offshore island moored in the Thames". Both are accurate descriptions.

The grandfather of New Labour architect Peter, now Lord, Mandelson was – in contrast to his grandson – a great opponent of the City of London. Herbert Morrison (later a minister in the Attlee government) writing in 1917 asked, "Is it not time London faced up to the pretentious buffoonery of the City of London Corporation? ... The City is now a square mile of entrenched reaction, the home of the devilry of modern finance".[9] Nearly one hundred years on, with the City of London even more powerful, it is time its powers were abolished, and the relatively few people who live there represented by one of the neighbouring local councils, who should take over the municipal functions, with the rest absorbed by the Mayor of London and the Greater London Assembly.

But tax avoidance is not just a problem of tax havens. There is also income shifting within companies which allows transnational corporations to avoid billions in tax. International accounting rules allow companies to report their results across the world as a single figure. As Nicholas Shaxson says, "as 60 per cent of world trade happens inside multinational corporations, this is massive opacity".[10] The global standard for corporate accounts reporting is the International Accounting Standards Board (IASB), which is not a body of the UN, IMF or World Bank, but a private company registered in Delaware, the tax haven US state. It is funded by the large accountancy firms and transnational corporations. Clearly, this will not do. But there is a simple solution, either nationally to pass laws requiring country-by-country reporting (so that companies have to report their results separately for each country of operation), or to act through larger bodies like the EU to create true global standards to stop governments being robbed of their tax revenues, leaving hard-pressed citizens to pick up the tab.

We must also consider some form of capital controls. These were a staple of the economic system from the end of the second world war until the 1970s and 80s when country after country abolished them (1979 in the UK, 1974 in the US and in the mid-1980s in France). In setting up that global financial system, John Maynard Keynes advocated capital controls should be a permanent feature. If we elect a government, shouldn't it control our currency rather than billionaire speculators or the equally unaccountable bond markets? One argument in favour of membership of the euro currency area was that its size made it less susceptible to market speculation, as happened to UK sterling in the early 1990s on a day known as 'Black Wednesday'.

While restoring some level of capital controls is one option, there are others. The US economist James Tobin advocated a tax on speculative financial transactions to make them unattractive. This has since been rebranded as the Robin Hood tax.[11] It is as much a 'sin tax' as it is a 'revenue tax'. The aim of sin taxes, like those on tobacco, alcohol, petrol or travelling into congested city centres, is to deter harmful actions. These may or may not have the effect of raising revenue, but their primary aim is to deter harmful activity. The Tobin or Robin Hood tax (also known as a financial transactions tax) is to deter speculative activity – the sort of socially useless activity that can increase the wealth of the speculators but can cause huge economic damage to nations' economies.

Such solutions of course require some sort of global agreement, which is why following the second world war the Bretton Woods agreements were signed establishing the rules of global finance and founding the World Bank and International Monetary Fund. Today, a group of nations is trying to build global agreement for a financial transactions tax. In the Eurozone, eleven countries (Austria, Belgium, Estonia, Finland, France, Germany, Greece, Italy, Portugal, Slovenia and Spain) have all signed up to a system of 'enhanced co-operation' to implement a financial transactions tax. It would work by taxing financial transactions in those member states. However, the UK government has refused to support and instead launched a legal challenge against it in the European Court of Justice, asserting that it would discriminate against UK financial companies (who would be taxed on their transactions in those countries). Again, we see our government acting on behalf of the financial sector rather than in the interests of us, its people. Another clear example occurred in 2013 when the chancellor George Osborne announced he would challenge in the European Court of Justice the EU's decision to cap bankers' bonuses at 100% of their basic salary. The cap is hardly stringent. Under the proposals, a banker earning £1 million a year could still receive an additional £1 million as a bonus (100% of salary). However, if the shareholders approved then the banker could receive up to 200% of their salary as a bonus. The UK chancellor, in post to run our economy in the public interest, opposes the rules he says "will make banks themselves riskier rather than safer" and is concerned that "increased disclosure of bankers' pay might breach individuals' right to privacy".[12] Of course, if bankers' salaries remain shrouded in secrecy then how are we to ever challenge them?

Many of the issues are global, but as we can see from the UK government's response to the financial transaction tax and bankers' bonus cap, it is often the UK that leads us in the wrong direction and is resistant to any global agreement. This is hardly surprising since at home too the UK government functions as servant to the finance sector.

In a democracy the most powerful interests must be democratically controlled or the term begins to lose its meaning.

Economic rights

If we aspire to a new democratic economy it must be accompanied by a new set of democratic rights. Having banks, energy companies, railways and more in public ownership in itself gives us greater democratic power. Having global agreements to limit the powers of speculators and the finance system is vital too.

But is public ownership itself sufficient? Even if we repeat the previous state-run nationalised model, then at least if the railways are badly managed or overly expensive we could vote out the government that made them so – just as in local elections we vote out councils that mismanage our refuse collection, libraries or social care facilities.

But there are alternative models of public ownership. Bob Crow, the late general secretary of the RMT rail workers' union, suggested that if the railways were brought back into public ownership they could be managed by a tri-partite board consisting equally of government (local and national), rail workers and industry representatives, and rail passengers.[13] Elected governments could delegate their representatives; workers could elect theirs through their unions and rail passengers could elect people to represent them in open elections. And there are many other models too, depending on what would be appropriate for each industry. For example, non-private UK housing has traditionally been council owned, rather than national, but there are models of co-operative ownership that are common and work effectively in other countries, including Sweden.

A new right to buy, and the right to sell

But why should our economic democratic rights end there. The Thatcher government introduced the right to buy (giving council tenants the right to buy the council house in which they lived at a heavy discount), but why not have that right extended to privately rented property too? Reflecting that many people now rent their housing not from the council but from private landlords. Conversely, should mortgage holders who get into financial trouble have the right to sell? If someone is at risk of losing their home as they can't keep up their mortgage payments, they could have the right to sell the property to the council, and the right to remain in it under an assured tenancy. The property would become a council home meaning the council gains an asset, and the householder stays in their home. All that would happen is a transaction between the council and the newly public bank offering the mortgage.

The right to buy-out

Corporate owners, as we noted in chapter four with the example of the Grangemouth oil refinery, can often make decisions in their interests that are in direct conflict with the public interest and the workers' interests. So workers should be given the right to buy too. If workers can raise the necessary funds they should have the right to buy out owners (with government subsidies to encourage). Such buy-outs could be collectively administered on workers' behalf through their trade unions, e.g. trade union members in favour could pay an additional levy into a hypothecated buy-out fund to raise money to buy-out owners.

Another variation on this model, could involve workers teaming up with regular customers to collectively raise the funds and then to jointly run the company in the interests of workers and customers.

The right to co-operativise

Another option would be to give workers the right to co-operativise their company – in other words to transfer the company from private ownership to co-operative. This could operate through a majority vote of workers, which if passed would give workers the right to co-operativise their company. Current owners could be compensated by the issuance of Treasury bonds – meaning that ownership of the company transferred to the state, but the day-to-day operation would be managed co-operatively by the workers.

Right to a citizen's income

The current reality of low paid work, life on a pension or on out of work benefits is poverty. That should not be the case – and in an economy anywhere near as developed as the UK, it need not be the case. The argument for a citizen's income, above the official poverty line, for every adult in the UK – would remove the need for separate benefits, means-testing, personal tax allowances, and the basic state pension.

A citizen's income would give people with ideas the ability to develop them and to start-up businesses and co-operatives more freely, to choose to work part-time or retire earlier (therefore freeing up work for others, necessary as technology limits the need for human input). A citizen's income is perfectly affordable – though it may require different choices about taxation levels, defence spending, etc. For pensioners, students, the unemployed, disabled people and low paid workers it is no less than the right to live free from poverty

Others suggest replacing the UK's poverty level minimum wage with a living wage. Economic modelling by the Institute for Fiscal Studies (IFS) in 2010 showed raising the minimum wage to the level of living wage would increase government revenues, through higher taxation payments and lower entitlement to in-work benefits. In turn, this extra government revenue could increase benefit and pension payments. Corporate low pay is effectively being subsidised by us all through tax credits and other payments.

Rights at work

With the technology available today, the fact that so many of us commute long distances with long journey times and still work five or six days per week is ludicrous. Why shouldn't the four or even three day week become the norm? Surely if mechanisation, robots and other technology is reducing or replacing the need for human input, then we should all share in that benefit, and all reduce our hours. The reality is that private ownership means that we don't, as those who own the banks, online retailers, supermarkets and factories pocket the savings of technology reducing or replacing labour.

One solution to this would be a proposal put by a candidate in the 2012 French Presidential election that profitable companies should not be allowed to make compulsory redundancies. After all, if the company is profitable what need is there to lay off staff? The provision does not of course preclude staff being retrained or moved into a different role to reflect changing business needs or practices. But what it shifts is the primary purpose of a business operation – from making profit for a few to ensuring stable employment (and therefore decent income) for many. Likewise, when technological advances necessitate fewer jobs, if the company remains profitable why not reduce working hours of staff while maintaining wage levels? Mark Serwotka, the general secretary of the PCS union, argues that we shouldn't "argue against technological advance, but to question who shares the proceeds of technological advance ... Do we as a society want to privilege the right of business owners to extract maximum profit above the rights of people to work, to get fair pay for that work and to have a healthy work-life balance". [14]

Conclusion

The suggestions laid out in this final chapter are not presented as a political programme, but a menu of policy options that politicians may consider should they wish to build an economy in the collective interest of the people. They are presented to show there is another way, a better way to run an economy, if we take the political decisions necessary to do so.

The sole focus of economic debate today seems to be about what leads to economic growth. But why are we so obsessed with economic growth? After all, growth measures the increase in gross domestic product (GDP), which is the value of all the goods and services produced which includes private and public consumption, government expenditure and investments, as well as exports less imports. In short, consuming more stuff, more economic activity equals growth. Measuring this is very difficult, as researchers at the Office for National Statistics will attest. So instead of measuring badly what matters less, why not prioritise measuring what matters most: the change in average living standards, whether inequality and poverty are reducing or increasing and whether unemployment is up or down. In a civilised society these things matter more.

The reality is though that even the best ideas will remain on paper unless we collectively develop them and campaign for them. Every democratic gain, every freedom from exploitation that has been won has been through organised collective action – and often in the face of ridicule and repression. But each movement – whether the suffragettes, the trade unionists, the anti-slavery campaigners and many more – all started with ideas being debated, discussed and improved, then campaigned for, often at first dismissed and rejected, and then won (at least in part).

Before universal suffrage, that great UK economist Adam Smith wrote in the Wealth of Nations that government is "in reality instituted for the defence of rich against poor". Today, we need economic democratic rights to ensure that our political rights aren't diminished by economic policies that prioritise the right to exploit others and to amass vast personal wealth.

Our responsibility today is to understand our economy and come up with better, fairer and more democratic ways of making it function. I hope this book is a contribution to that task, even if only that it makes you come up with something better or join with others to campaign for a change you feel passionately about.

This book unashamedly lays the blame for the UK economy at the feet of politicians, but there are political solutions, if we make them happen. Continue the debate with me via twitter @ AndrewFisher79 or email andrewfisher1979@gmail.com

Endnotes

Chapter 1: The financial crash – what happened?

1   This scheme covered the first £35,000 in a depositor's account. This was later raised to £50,000 (from 30 June 2009) and then £85,000 (from 31 December 2010)

2   See more at http://www.taxresearch.org.uk/Blog/2008/02/20/ northern-rock-why-granite-must-be-nationalised/ (retrieved on 10/02/13)

3   Cited in Sikka, P. Financial Crisis and the silence of the auditors. Accounting, Organizations and Society 34 (2009) pp.868-873

4   Treasury Select Committee report, 24 January 2008. The run on the Rock. p.115

5   Sikka, P. Financial Crisis and the silence of the auditors. Accounting, Organizations and Society 34 (2009) pp.868-873

6   Budget speech, 21 March 2007

7   It is interesting that in many religions, usury – lending money with interest – is either forbidden or condemned in the texts of Hinduism, Buddhism, Judaism, Christianity, and Islam. Not much unites religions, but condemnation of usury appears universal.

8   Murphy, R. 'Network Banking: a radical solution for the banking crisis' IN: Fisher, A (ed). November 2008. LEAP Red Papers: the economic crisis. LEAP, London

9　New Economics Foundation. 'Where does money come from?' December 2012. Retrieved from http://www.neweconomics. org/publications/where-does-money-come-from on 16 February 2012

10　A CDO squared is effectively a bundle of bundled-up mortgages (CDOs)

11　Griffin, J & Tang, D.Y. Did Credit Rating Agencies Make Unbiased Assumptions on CDOs? American Economic Review: Papers & Proceedings 2011, 101:3, 125–130

12　HSBC. February 2012. Savings Map of Britain. Retrieved from http://www.newsroom.hsbc.co.uk%2Farticles%2Fsavings_ intentions_for_2012%2Fattachment&ei=ayAhUYOnLcXctAbu vIGgBg&usg=AFQjCNE7BdH6IeZEEtv7d7KGmv5mg8bhog& bvm=bv.42553238,d.d2k&cad=rja on 13 February 2013

13　According to Mick Brooks, in his book Capitalist Crisis, theory and practice. 2012, expedia, London

14　Speech made on 21 October 2008 in Leeds

15　Quoted in Sikka, P. Financial Crisis and the silence of the auditors. Accounting, Organizations and Society 34 (2009) pp.868-873

Chapter 2: Sowing the seeds

1　Lawson, N. 1992. The View from No.11. Transworld Publishers, London p.65

2　Figures given by then Chancellor Norman Lamont in a parliamentary answer, cited in Hansard: HC Deb 03 March 1992 vol 205 c123W

3　Quoted in McDonnell, J. 2007. Another World is Possible. LRC, London

4　Lawson, N. 1992. The View from No.11. Transworld Publishers, London p.985

5　Riddell, P. 1989. The Thatcher Decade: How Britain Has

Changed During the 1980s. Blackwell, Oxford p.88

6   Benn, T. 1995. The Benn Diaries: new single volume edition. Arrow Books, London p.421

7   Lawson, N. 1992. The View from No.11. Transworld Publishers, London p.34

8   Quoted in Morning Star 13 October 2009 'Brown's £16bn assets fire sale'.

9   Lawson, N. 1992. The View from No.11. Transworld Publishers, London p.201

10 Lawson, N. 1992. The View from No.11. Transworld Publishers, London p.234

11 Both opinion polls cited in Hall, D & Lobina, E. April 2008. Water Privatisation. Public Services International Research Unit (PSIRU), University of Greenwich

12 YouGov polling for the Class thinktank 27-28 October 2013. Published at: http://classonline.org.uk/docs/Class-YouGov_poll_results_28_October_2013.pdf. Retrieved on 31/12/13

13 Data from ONS: Share Ownership, 2010. 28 February 2012

14 Data from DWP: Second Tier Pension Provision. Calculations are author's own.

15 in conversation with the author.

16 Murphy, R. Making Pensions Work. Finance for the Future, October 2010

17 Lawson, N. 1992. The View from No.11. Transworld Publishers, London p.239

18 Figures from the King's Fund

19 Investigation by the Daily Mirror, published on 05/03/13 under the headline 'Great Tory housing shame: Third of ex-council homes now owned by rich landlords'. Retrieved from http://www.mirror.co.uk/news/uk-news/right-to-buy-housing-shame-third-ex-council-1743338 on 07/12/13

20 Data from Nationwide Building Society: Real House Prices – 1975-2012

21 According to survey data by LSL Property Services, 2012

22 Nigel Lawson, Mais lecture 1984

23 Lawson, N. 1992. The View from No.11. Transworld Publishers, London p.432

24 Lawson, N. 1992. The View from No.11. Transworld Publishers, London p.437

25 Quoted in Boffey, D. 'Recession is a good time to boost profits, says Cameron aide'. Observer, 12/05/13

26 PCS. 2010. There is an Alternative: the case against cuts in public spending. PCS, London.

27 Lawson, N. 1992. The View from No.11. Transworld Publishers, London p.439

28 Fisher, A. The National Minimum Wage: when an increase is a cut. LEAP blog, 15 April 2013. Retrieved from http://leap-lrc. blogspot.co.uk/2013/04/the-national-minimum-wage-when-increase.html on 09/11/13

29 Lawson, N. 1992. The View from No.11. Transworld Publishers, London p.35

30 Lawson, N. 1992. The View from No.11. Transworld Publishers, London p.36

31 Speech made by Nigel Lawson to the Zurich Society of Economics at the Kongresshaus, Zurich, on Wednesday 14 January 1981

32 15 Mar 1988 – Hansard

33 See Emmerson, C & Tetlow, G. 'Pensions and Retirement Policy – 2010 Election Briefing Note No.16'. Institute for Fiscal Studies. p.4

34 Lawson, N. 1992. The View from No.11. Transworld Publishers, London p.90

35 Calculation by author, using HM Treasury data

36 Hansard, House of Commons, 21 March 2012 Col 802-3

37 Lawson, N. 1992. The View from No.11. Transworld Publishers, London p.351

38 Lawson, N. 1992. The View from No.11. Transworld Publishers, London p.353

39 See Bank of England chart in Lawson, N. 1992. The View from No.11. Transworld Publishers, London p.980

40 Lyons, J. 'Millionaire Tory minister wants UK to be a "tax haven" for the super rich'. The Mirror, 07/04/12. Retrieved from http://www.mirror.co.uk/news/uk-news/francis-maude-wants-uk-to-be-a-tax-783595 on 06/12/13

41 Gordon Brown's Mansion House speech, 22 June 2006

42 Lawson, N. 1992. The View from No.11. Transworld Publishers, London p.342

43 Shaxson, N. 2011. Treasure Islands. Vintage Books, London p.16

44 Lawson, N. 1992. The View from No.11. Transworld Publishers, London p.39

45 Hansard, House of Lords, 7 November 1979, Col 891

46 Lawson, N. 1992. The View from No.11. Transworld Publishers, London p.736

47 Lawson, N. 1992. The View from No.11. Transworld Publishers, London p.1023

48 Lawson, N. 1992. The View from No.11. Transworld Publishers, London p.627

49 Lawson, N. 1992. The View from No.11. Transworld Publishers, London p.401

50 Lawson, N. 1992. The View from No.11. Transworld Publishers, London p.412

51 Lawson, N. 1992. The View from No.11. Transworld Publishers, London p.1026

52 Speech to CBI conference in 2005

53 Cited in Shaxson, N. 2011. Treasure Islands. Vintage Books, London

54 [1]Jones, R. October 2013. SPERI Paper No.6 – The UK's Innovation Deficit & How to Repair it. Sheffield Political Economy Research Institute. p.3

55 Data from ONS, UK GDP since 1955; calculation author's own

Chapter 3: The Illusion of an economy

1   See Turner, G. 2008. 2009. No Way to Run an Economy. Pluto Press, London, p.102

2   Lawson, N. 1992. The View from No.11. Transworld Publishers, London p.56

3   See cabinet papers released under the thirty year rule in January 2014. Reported by Higham, N. 03/01/14. 'Cabinet papers reveal 'secret coal pits closure plan'. BBC News website. Retrieved from http://www.bbc.co.uk/news/uk-25549596 on 10/01/14

4   Lawson, N. 1992. The View from No.11. Transworld Publishers, London p.858

5   Lawson, N. 1992. The View from No.11. Transworld Publishers, London p.868

6   Lawson, N. 1992. The View from No.11. Transworld Publishers, London p.423

7   Lawson, N. 1992. The View from No.11. Transworld Publishers, London p.421

8   Lawson, N. 1992. The View from No.11. Transworld Publishers, London p.813

9   Lawson, N. 1992. The View from No.11. Transworld Publishers, London p.977

10 HM Treasury figures 'T11.11 Government revenues from UK oil and gas production'. Retrieved from http://www.hmrc.gov.uk/statistics/prt/table11-11.pdf on 13/12/13

11 [1]Elliot, L.29 March 2012. 'Britain has squandered golden opportunity North Sea oil promised'. Guardian Economics Blog: http://www.guardian.co.uk/business/economics-blog/2012/mar/29/north-sea-oil-revenue-squandered (retrieved on 21/06/13)

12 Conway, E. 'North Sea oil is dragging us into the red'. Daily

Telegraph, 5 November 2009

13 According to forecasts in HM Treasury, Autumn Statement 2013, CM8747

14 Cited in Larry Elliott. 'UK's £10tn debt timebomb could harm economy for decades, study says'. The Guardian, 09/11/10. Retrieved on 07/12/13 from: http://www.theguardian.com/business/2010/nov/09/debt-timebomb-harm-economy-decades

15 Turner, G. 2009, No Way to Run an Economy. Pluto Press, London p. 112

16 Mellows-Facer, A & Maer, L. 27 January 2012. 'International comparisons of manufacturing output. House of Commons Library, London p.4

17 Lawson, N. 1992. The View from No.11. Transworld Publishers, London p.632

18 Lawson, N. 1992. The View from No.11. Transworld Publishers, London p.630

19 Lawson, N. 1992. The View from No.11. Transworld Publishers, London p.806

20 Shaxson, N. 2011. Treasure Islands. Vintage Books, London pp.vii-viii

21 John McDonnell MP interviewed by Dermot Murnaghan on the Sky News Channel, 8 October 2008. View full interview online at: http://www.youtube.com/watch?gl=GB&hl=en-GB&v=8-ClxSf3z4k

22 See http://www.actionaid.org.uk/news-and-views/barclays-must-stop-promoting-the-use-of-tax-havens-in-africa-actionaid-report. Retrieved on 13/12/13

23 See http://www.hsgac.senate.gov/subcommittees/investigations/media/hsbc-exposed-us-finacial-system-to-money-laundering-drug-terrorist-financing-risks. Retrieved on 13/12/13

24 Data from EBA report 'High Earners 2012 data'. European Banking Authority, London. Calculations are author's own

25 Keynes, JM. 1933. National Self-sufficiency (section 3)

Chapter 4: The state of our economy

1   Speech by the governor of the Bank of England in Edinburgh, 20 October 2009. Retrieved from http://www.theguardian.com/business/2009/oct/21/mervyn-king-attack-banks-bailout

2   Figures from European Banking Federation, EBF Banking Statistics Database 2012. Retrieved from http://www.ebf-fbe.eu/uploads/2012%20-New%20BankStat%20Database.xls on 14/12/13. Calculations author's own.

3   [1]Jones, R. October 2013. SPERI Paper No.6 – The UK's Innovation Deficit & How to Repair it. Sheffield Political Economy Research Institute. p.3

4   See ONS. Balance of Payments, Q3 2013. ONS Statistical Bulletin, London. Retrieved from http://www.ons.gov.uk/ons/dcp171778_347294.pdf on 05/01/14

5   OECD data, cited in Baker, D. Attacking the Treasury View, Again. CEPR, Washington DC, June 2012. p.5

6   Data from 'Annex d: OBR's Economic and fiscal outlook: selected tables' in Budget report 2012. Retrieved from http://webarchive.nationalarchives.gov.uk/20130129110402/http://cdn.hm-treasury.gov.uk/budget2012_annexd.pdf on 14/12/13. Calculations are author's own.

7   Source: HM Treasury, Public Finances Databank, http://www.hm-treasury.gov.uk/d/public_finances_databank.xls. The apparent increase in investment in the 2000s (relative to the 1980s and 1990s) is partially explained by the sharply reduced size of the economy after 2008 as a result of the economic crash.

8   Figures by Mark Helowell. 'Shovel ready?'. Public Finance magazine, October 2013, pp25-29

9   See Mazzucato, M. 2013. The Entrepreneurial State. Anthem Press, London

10 Jacobs, E. GPS, lithium batteries, the internet, cellular technology, airbags: A Q&A about how governments often fuel innovation.

Retrieved from http://blog.ted.com/2013/10/28/qa-mariana-mazzucato-governments-often-fuel-innovation/ on 31/12/13

11 See Thornton, J. Bite the Bullet Train. Public Finance magazine, December 2013. Retrieved from http://www.publicfinance. co.uk/features/2013/12/bite-the-bullet-train/ on 30/12/13

12 According to research by the Centre for Research on Socio-Cultural Change (Cresc) cited in Chakrabortty, A. ' Rail privatisation: legalised larceny'. The Guardian, 04/11/13. Retrieved from http://www.theguardian.com/ commentisfree/2013/nov/04/rail-privatisation-train-operators-profit on 30/12/13

13 See YouGov polling for the Class thinktank 27-28 October 2013. Published at: http://classonline.org.uk/docs/Class-YouGov_poll_results_28_October_2013.pdf. Retrieved on 31/12/13

14 Enerdata. Global Energy Statistical Yearbook 2013. Data retrieved from http://yearbook.enerdata.net/#renewable-data-in-world-primary-consumption-shares-by-region.html on 31/12/13

15 Baker, D. Attacking the Treasury View, Again. CEPR, Washington DC, June 2012. p.6

16 Cited in Islam, F. 'Home Ownership: how the property dream turned into a nightmare'. Observer, 18/08/13

17 See DCLG. Feb 2013. English Housing Survey 2011 to 2012: headline report. DCLG, London

18 Intergenerational Foundation. 2013. 'Why BTL equals Big Tax Let-off'. IF, London

19 PCS. Britain needs a pay rise. PCS, London. Retrieved from http://pcs.org.uk/en/news_and_events/news_centre/index.cfm/id/5E952460-5E11-4C8B-8049A74DF8EA756F on 12/02/13

20 Data from TUC. 'The Great Wages Grab'. TUC, London Retrieved from http://www.tuc.org.uk/sites/default/files/tucfiles/TheGreatWagesGrab.pdf on 31/12/13

21 Quoted in Elliott, L. 'Analysis: why more jobs may reflect hard times for workers'. The Guardian, 03/12/12

22 Cited in chart from Lloyd, C., Mason, G. and Mayhew, K. (2008) (eds) Low-Wage Work in the United Kingdom. New York: Russell Sage Foundation.

23 John Schmitt. 2012. Low Wage Lessons. Retrieved from http://www.cepr.net/documents/publications/low-wage-2012-01.pdf on 21/12/13

24 Figures from the OECD, 2011

25 IFS. Average private incomes fall over 7% in the three years to 2010-11. IFS, London, 15 June 2013.

26 See Dorling, D. March 2012. The case for austerity among the rich. IPPR, London

27 Figures cited in Dorling, D. March 2012. The case for austerity among the rich. IPPR, London

28 Cited in Shaxson, N. 2011. Treasure Islands. Vintage Books, London p.27

29 Orwell, G. 1937. The Road to Wigan Pier. Victor Gollancz, London

30 More commonly known as 'final salary' or 'career average' pension schemes. These enable the scheme member to calculate what their pension will be, and therefore to plan their retirement.

31 Figures quoted in PCS, NPC, Unite, NUT, UCU. 2011.'Fair Pensions for All'. PCS, London

32 Quoted in Jones, R ' Household finances at breaking point, says Shelter'. The Guardian. 03/01/14. Retrieved from http://www.theguardian.com/money/2014/jan/03/household-finances-breaking-point-shelter on 05/01/14

33 Harriet Harman delivering the Charles Wheeler Lecture on journalism at the University of Westminster, 13 June 2013

34 Quoted in an interview in The Financial Times with David Wighton who informs Mandelson apparently "added hurriedly", "as long as they pay their taxes". 'Mandelson plans a microchip off the old block', FT, 23 October 1998.

35 Budget Statement, March 2012

36 Quoted in Lyons, J. 'Millionaire Tory minister wants UK to be a "tax haven" for the super rich'. The Mirror 07/04/12. Retrieved from http://www.mirror.co.uk/news/uk-news/francis-maude-wants-uk-to-be-a-tax-783595 on 30/12/13

37 Marina Hyde. ' Who would credit the word of banking's knights-erroneous?'. The Guardian, 14/02/09. Retrieved from http://www.theguardian.com/commentisfree/2009/feb/14/marina-hyde on 13/12/13

38 Quoted in the Daily Telegraph, 18 July 2012. 'HSBC money-laundering scandal casts a cloud over Lord Green, the trade minister'. Stephen Green was Group Chief Executive of HSBC from 1 June 2003, and became HSBC chairman from 1 January 2005 until December 2010.

Chapter 5: Building an economy that works

1 somewhat interrupted by the birth of my first child, and then constantly yet wonderfully interrupted since, it has to be confessed

2 Cited in Cahill, K. 2002. Who owns Britain? Canongate Books, Edinburgh

3 Wetzel, D. 16/12/09. 'The UK needs annual land value tax'. Retrieved from http://leap-lrc.blogspot.co.uk/2009/12/uk-needs-annual-land-value-tax.html on 09/01/13

4 For more information on land value tax, see http://labourland.org/

5 Cited in Shaxson, N. 2011. Treasure Islands. Vintage Books, London p.77

6 The governor of the Bank of England must write a letter to the Chancellor if inflation rises above 2%, setting out the reasons for this and what the Bank will do to get inflation heading towards 2%

7 Quoted in McKinsey Global Institute discussion paper: 'QE and

ultra-low interest rates: Distributional effects and risks'. McKinsey & Company, November 2013. See chart on p.17

8   For an excellent account of how tax havens and financial secrecy shield terrorist funding, see Napoleoni, L. 2005. Terror Incorporated. Seven Stories Press, New York

9   Cited in Shaxson, N. 2011. Treasure Islands. Vintage Books, London p.260

10 Shaxson, N. 2011. Treasure Islands. Vintage Books, London p.251

11 See http://robinhoodtax.org.uk/ for more information about the campaign.

12 Cited in Stewart, H. Osborne bats for bankers' bonuses citing risk to City from EU cap. The Guardian, 25/09/13. Retrieved from http://www.theguardian.com/politics/2013/sep/25/osborne-bankers-bonuses-eu-cap on 30/12/13

13 See Crow, B. 'Rail privatisation – a failed experiment' in Fisher, A (ed). 2008. Building the new common sense: social ownership for the 21st century'. LEAP, London

14 Serwotka, M. January 2013. Beyond Capitalism? A Lecture. Plymouth Business School, Plymouth

Index

Publishers Announcement

The Failed Experiment is the first book published under our new Radical Read imprint.

The underlying theme in the Radical Read series is to question why challenging ideas and causes, that once fuelled a great movement, have been stifled by a narrow political elite. We intend to offer books on contemporary issues written in a lively style that aim to be informative, thought provoking and precise.

We are inviting organisations interested in this project to become Associate Partners, with an opportunity to participate in the Radical Read project. Enabling them to suggest new titles, review pre-publication manuscripts, monitor policy and share research facilities.

We are always interested in hearing from Authors with something to say and opinions backed by hard facts.

And of course we want readers to keep in touch and offer suggestions for books.

Please visit our website http://www.radicalread.co.uk/

Comerford and Miller
Progressive Publishers